Mommy! Daddy! I'm Afraid!

Mommy! Daddy! I'm Afraid!

HELP YOUR CHILDREN OVERCOME FEARS THAT HOLD THEM BACK IN SCHOOL AND AT PLAY

Stephen M. Joseph

COLLIER BOOKS
A DIVISION OF MACMILLAN PUBLISHING CO., INC.
NEW YORK

With few exceptions, I've changed names and places and altered events to preserve the privacy and keep the confidence of the people in this book from whom I learned so much.

Macmillan Publishing Co., Inc.
866 Third Avenue, New York, N.Y. 10022
Collier Macmillan Canada, Ltd.

Library of Congress Cataloging in Publication Data
Joseph, Stephen M., 1938-
Mommy! Daddy! I'm afraid!
Reprint of the ed. published by Holt, Rinehart and Winston under title: Children in fear.
1. Fear in children. I. Title.
BF723.F4J6 1979 155.4'18 78-26029
ISBN 0-02-043930-X

First Collier Books Edition 1979

Mommy! Daddy! I'm Afraid! was originally published in a hardcover edition under the title *Children in Fear* by Holt, Rinehart and Winston.

Printed in the United States of America

Grateful acknowledgment is made for permission to reprint "New Fangled Preacher Man," words by Peter Udell, music by Gary Geld, from the Broadway musical *Purlie* copyright © 1970 Mourbar Music Corp./Belack Music Corp./ Udell Music Company/Geld Music Company.

This book is dedicated to my friend and teacher, Denah Harris, who encouraged me to begin it and helped me to complete it, and to my daughter Allison, with love, hope, and joy.

Don't be afraid to face facts, and never lose your ability to ask the questions: Why? and How? Be in this like a child. In religion, the great revelations and the great authorities—the founding fathers—belong to the past, and the older the authority, the greater it is. In science, unlike religion, the great revolutions lie in the future; the coming generations are the authorities; and the pupil is greater than the master, if he has the gift to see things anew.

—Immanuel Velikovsky

What is most surprising of all is how much fear there is in school. Why is so little said about it? Perhaps most people do not recognize fear in children when they see it. They can read the grossest signs of fear; they know what the trouble is when a child clings howling to his mother; but the subtler signs of fear escape them. It is these signs, in children's faces, voices and gestures, in their movements and ways of working, that tell me plainly that most children in school are scared most of the time, many of them very scared.

—John Holt

CONTENTS

A NOTE TO THE READER

Young children are afraid most of the time, so afraid that they find it difficult to learn, to think, and to grow. I didn't know this until quite recently, though I've spent most of the past ten years as a teacher. It's been the last two years, working with twenty-three preschool children, which convinced me.

While compiling and editing *The Me Nobody Knows,* my awareness of children's thinking began to expand enormously. As a teacher in ghetto schools, I experienced the children's exuberant vitality and hopefulness, though later I learned to see and hear their desperation as well. But with their inner strength there was a fear of other people and of the world around them, behind them, and ahead of them. Their writing ached and screamed with fear, but why were these children so afraid? Was it solely the poverty and violence in their lives? Or were middle-class children equally afraid of different things . . . or the same things? Were all children, of all ages and classes, afraid?

Many adults seem to be constantly fearful, too. Did they learn this fear as children? I don't mean the rational fear of touching a hot stove, or of running out into the traffic, or of losing one's job, but the pervasive, crippling fear of new experiences, of other people as the enemy, of punishment for making mistakes or raising questions in taboo areas, and of death and punishment, both real and symbolic, fears that haunt our dreams, asleep and awake.

Most of my teaching experience had been with early adolescents who were reluctant to speak about their fears, though they occasionally wrote about them. They were afraid to admit they were afraid. In nursery schools, though, I found that young children still felt free enough to share their thoughts and apprehensions. I tried to understand what makes them afraid, what made me afraid when I was their age, and what I could do to help them.

We'd like to think that children are happy, but most are not. They are obsessed. This, then, is a book about obsessive fears; theirs, mine, and perhaps yours. I set out to learn which fears and behavior problems are taught to children, and which, if any, are instinctual. I wanted to learn to solve life's problems constructively. From birth, I'd been taught to think of these problems as insolvable. I realize that as a child, I wondered: Why are people called bad and good? Why do people punish each other, sometimes with death? Is death a punishment? Is it a punishment for bad people, for bad children? Are people really born bad and good, or are they just taught to be cruel and destructive to each other?

I was unwilling to adjust, to learn to live with these problems, because this seemed to me to rob life of any meaning or rational purpose. The further I pursued these questions, though, the more I became aware that I was afraid, too, and had been all of my life. I've written this book, not only to help children and their parents, but to learn about my own fears, and what I could do about the fundamental human problems that lie behind them.

In *Children in Fear,* I've explored aspects of a scientific theory of human nature developed by a psychiatric social worker named Denah Harris. My earlier experiences as a teacher, gathering material for *The Me Nobody Knows,* had prepared me to be receptive to her ideas. Harris's theory intrigued me because one of its major objectives was the relief of irrational fear. Her evidence suggested that she had helped her clients to solve problems they'd previously thought of as hopeless.* I began to be convinced of Harris's statement that I had been educated to a *theory* about human nature, the moral theory, which holds that human beings are born embodying good and evil, should be rewarded and punished accordingly by God and each other, and would die for their sins, consciously experiencing the pain of being dead—hence, a living death. This term, moral theory, comes up repeatedly in *Children in Fear*. The concepts *good* and *bad* derive from moral theories about human nature which may not be accurate. The comprehension of these concepts is critical to understanding why I related to the children as I did. I believe my data about the experiences of very young children involved in their primary explorations of a terrifying world and its problems show the crippling effects of the assumptions of that theory. These children were born into a world that categorizes them as little monsters who need to be civilized.

In contrast, I based my work with these children on the idea that there is no innate evil in any child—or in any adult. For that matter neither is there good. What is it then which causes adults to relate to children and each other *as if* they were dangerous combinations of good and evil? It seems that most of us were taught these contradictions by our schools, our families, our religions, the entertainment media; indeed, by the entire culture.

The techniques for solving problems in *Children in Fear*,

* As far as possible, I've limited the scope of this book to my own experiences. Denah Harris is preparing the theory of human nature, Corticology, which she has developed. However, her help was invaluable in planning and carrying out this work, which has been an essential step in my own reeducation.

which are designed especially to help parents, are based on a way of thinking about children which I've reiterated many times, in as many ways as I could within the chapters. For example, I learned to interpret many of the children's actions and statements as *questions* about themselves and the people around them. The following pages explore the questions we asked each other—the children, their parents, their teachers, and me—and the answers we began to discover together.

I ask you to forgive me if I seem redundant. Most people are willing to listen endlessly to stories about good and evil, but I realize that unfamiliar terms like problem-solver and cortex, often repeated, can soon sound doctrinaire. We need to work together to develop a vocabulary which reflects this new way of looking at children.

Some readers may think I've exaggerated the children's obsessional preoccupation with death and death games. I worked primarily in an unstructured classroom; unstructured but not unsupervised. Most of the games, by far, that the children played, dealt with death. No one told them which games to play, so they made up their own. In structured classrooms, although the concern with death is just as present, there is little opportunity to play these games, and the concern is far less directly expressed.

Other readers may think that these children are unusually violent because they live in New York City, and New York is not typical of the rest of the world, or even the United States. New York may be special, but if you think these children and their problems are atypical, sit unobtrusively in any playground, anywhere, and observe children who are playing without supervision, or ask to observe in a nursery school where unstructured play is permitted. I think you'll see essentially what I saw.

It's also true that most children act differently in school; they act out problems and questions which they'd be afraid to ask at home. The children I worked with used four-letter words with me that they rarely used around other adults. I think it's because they thought I would tell them why those words were taboo, what they meant, and also to test out if I really wouldn't punish them for this.

As both a parent and a teacher, I know how hard it is at times for all of us. We parents often find it all we can do to survive. Our complex society offers little help and few supports and creates far too many obstacles; in these circumstances, it seems impossible to be constantly aware of our children's needs. Our culture hasn't yet established the priority of children's learning.

Please remember that it's all right to make mistakes; they are part of learning. Teach that to your children, too. The techniques I used with the children can be used by anyone. There's no magic involved, but it is imporant to be consistent. If you try problem-solving once, and it doesn't work, that doesn't mean it won't work the next time, or the time after that. We can't expect total success since there is an entire culture working against us, reinforcing the idea in children's minds that they, and everyone else are sometimes good but mostly bad and will be punished for their sins.

Being a parent is probably the most difficult and important work anyone can undertake. As parents, we hope for a rational world where children can expect empathy from us and each other, and where there are no enemies. Ultimately, that will be up to them, but we can help. The hope of this book then, is that we parents can do something *more*. Perhaps we can change the lives of our families by trying these ideas and techniques. It would be a new beginning.

ACKNOWLEDGMENTS

My special thanks to my wife, Barbara, for her constant, loving support, for encouraging me to explore questions and ideas I hadn't been able to think about since my childhood, for convincing me that the struggle to think is the first step to change, and for reading and rereading this manuscript with a sharp pencil and great tenderness.

My thanks to parents, children, and teachers, particularly Susanah Doyle, Claudia DiRosa Turner, Fleda Tiggs, and of course, Denah Harris.

Thank you Tom Carew, Kingsley Eaton, Flora Davis, John and Naomi Holland, Stanley Marcus, Ron Turner, and Richard Zucker for your help with the earlier versions of this manuscript.

My thanks, also, to my editors Joseph Cunneen and Elisabeth Scharlatt for all of their support.

It would be impossible to separately thank everyone who helped me, and to all of you, . . . I'm deeply grateful.

Mommy! Daddy! I'm Afraid!

1

The Oldest Boy in the Class

In one corner of the large room, two golden-haired four-year-old girls sat flanking a dark child with a soft lamb's-wool Afro. They were reading a Dr. Dolittle book, helping each other with the difficult words, laughing with recognition at the illustrations from the movie they'd all seen.

Four boys of about the same age, in overalls and flannel shirts, sat directly across the room, modeling figures out of clay which they first punched with their fists. When they finished a model, they pretended to fly it, as if it were a toy airplane.

Another group of children played with water, soap, and vegetable coloring in the sink. Their voices were high pitched and excited as they filled plastic bottles with the mixture.

At the foot of a jungle gym, in the shadow of pillows larger than a child, another group of girls used an upside-down cardboard carton to play house. Near them, a big-eyed, curly-haired boy in a Superman T-shirt told a story to two friends who listened intently as they stared at him.

The three girls in the corner were reading about Dr. Dolittle throwing a seal—disguised as an old lady—over a cliff, so that she could swim north to her mate. Otherwise, she tells the Doctor, he "would die, or have a nervous breakdown, if he didn't see me."

The seal swims away but Dr. Dolittle is observed by workmen, who report him to the police. He is arrested and charged with murder by a cruel judge. An animal tells Dr. Dolittle some unsavory secrets about the judge's private life. Dolittle threatens the judge who relents, but threatens to commit Dolittle to a mental institution. Dolittle escapes from prison and boards a ship, but the ship is wrecked near a desert island, to which he and the captain row. On the island they discover a tribe of black natives with bones through their noses, whom they first mystify, and then subjugate.

The girls understood most of the words and seemed to enjoy the story, but they appeared to be worried about some of the adventures. It was clear that they didn't really know it was "just a story": they thought it was true.

The four boys began to throw their clay figures at each other.

"This is how Gigantor murdered those yucky Russians yesterday," Ken said. "He killed them with his fire ray!"

Eddie and Glen crashed their clay figures head-on.

"My monster is the strongest in the world. What he wants he takes, and if nobody don't like it, he burns off their heads!" Glen said.

"Yeah, mine, too," Terry whispered to himself, putting toothpicks in his figure's forehead. "When I finish this Gigantor, he's gonna run all yours through with his bayonet head. He'll cut you to ribbons!"

"O.K.," Marky shouted to Philip and Andrew, "move closer to the sink, and put some more soap in the bottles. If you want to play with me, you gotta make more bottles of poison potion. There's a lotta kids in this class we gotta poison!"

"But I don't want to poison anyone," Andrew protested, frowning and looking worried.

"Who cares what you want?" Marky screamed. "If you don't listen to me, I'll bring a bomb to your house and blow it up, and I'm not kidding, either! I got a whole bunch of bombs at home. My father brings them from work." Andrew's face paled, and he began to cry.

Inside the cardboard carton, Carrie and Anne were spanking Doris, the "baby."

"Bad, bad, bad!" Carrie yelled, "Wait till Daddy gets home. He'll beat you till you bleed. He'll kick your ass!"

"Quiet!" Bobby hissed from the other side of the jungle gym. "I'm trying to finish my story about the mugging." He turned back to Freddy and Sean, who waited for him to finish.

"Anyway," he said, "he grabbed the old man around the throat. Then he knocked him down and kicked him in the head. The old man was yelling 'Help, police!' but my mommy said, 'Let's get the Hell out of here.' She hurt my arm pulling me across the street!"

It was a typical morning in nursery school, a routine day. These were normal children in a conventional class. No one has categorized them as disturbed, and theirs is a fine private school which most parents would be proud to have their sons and daughters attend. Nevertheless, scenes like the previous ones, with variations, are played out at this school every day, and in many nursery schools and kindergartens across the country.

We think of nursery school as a place where children learn to play with each other, to share, to make friends, to differ, to fight, and to make up. They did all of this, but with a degree of violence and fear I didn't imagine or anticipate. It wasn't the amount of conflict that surprised me, but the nature of that conflict.

Instead of being friends, the children were more often mistrustful and unable to count on their classmates. I expected the nursery school to be a peaceful place—not quiet; young children shouldn't have to be quiet—but different somehow from the world outside. I discovered it isn't different; it's a microcosm of the larger world. Conflict between the children didn't lead to the solution of problems, but rather to the resigned conviction that problems couldn't be solved. I had hoped the nursery school would be an oasis; instead I found a training ground for fear.

The nursery school where I did most of my work occupies the two top floors of a gray Victorian church in Manhattan. The church has beautiful rose windows but the building itself, and the next-door rectory, are dark and gloomy.

The entrance to the school is through a black wrought-iron gate, and along a cement walk flanked by low stone walls and a privet hedge. The rectory's big wooden doors are double-locked every night, against the desperation of neighborhood drug addicts. During the time I spent at the school, the building was broken into five times. One teacher was robbed at gunpoint; other teachers' handbags were stolen while they were in class with the children.

I worked with a teacher named Marilyn Benetti. To get to her classroom, which was called the Penthouse, I climbed two flights of damp-smelling, blue slate stairs. They spiraled through thick brick walls, and echoed like the steps leading to a dungeon. On the landings, small windows let in cold squares of light. Each quarter hour, the church bells rang out the time.

Marilyn's classroom was bright and airy, unlike the rest of the building. Under the very high ceiling there were lots of long windows, and warm, faded rugs covered the marble floor. Children's paintings hung on the freshly painted walls. There were terrariums and aquariums on top of the low shelves, filled with very green weeds, gerbils, goldfish, and an occasional frog.

In one corner there was a wooden jungle gym; in another, an easel and paints. The third corner held a bookcase full of blocks, and in the fourth corner was the doorway. The room was divided into areas by low bookcases. It was a Montessori school, which means that the equipment and furniture are child-sized. Some of the small bookcases were arranged to make a reading corner, with large cushions to lie on and small chairs for sitting.

The shelves were filled with Montessori materials—beads to count with, puzzles, games, and equipment that taught the children to recognize different textures and even to tie bows. The Montessori Method tries to provide a rich environment for children. Theoretically, there should always be something stimulating for them to do, to explore, and to master, but many five- and six-year-olds, after spending two years at the school, felt they had exhausted the available materials.*

Marilyn was small, soft-spoken, and self-assured. She had two assistants, a dark and beautiful young woman in African dress named Eileen and a pale bearded young man in shoulder length hair named Phil.

I spent an afternoon with Marilyn exchanging ideas about children and learning. We agreed that fear might have a powerful effect on children's ability to learn and to live. I told her I was exploring an aspect of Denah Harris's theory; that human beings are potentially perfect problem-solvers

* Though this school was chartered by the American Montessori Association, it was very loosely structured. What I observed there hardly varied from the many other non-Montessori nursery schools I visited and observed in.

because of their innate physiological equipment. I thought I could discover from observing young children where they learned to be afraid, and explore Harris's theory with them so that they might learn to be less fearful.

Marilyn was always open and ready to explore. "I could use some new information," she conceded. "Things are happening in my classroom that I don't understand. Disturbing things—constant fighting, name-calling, children terrorizing other children. The children are upset by it, and so am I. I'm not sure what to do about it. If you think you can help, come as often as you like."

From then on, I came every day. It was the middle of the term, so the children already knew the teachers and each other. I sat in a child-sized chair against the wall and tried to be unobtrusive. This was difficult, since I'm 6′3″, and had a red beard and moustache—hardly a typical nursery school visitor.

Marilyn introduced me simply as Steve and told the children that I would be visiting with them. She didn't say for how long, because at the time neither of us really knew. For the first two weeks I just sat and watched them—twenty-four children, from almost four to almost six years old, thirteen boys and eleven girls, dressed mostly in overalls and pants. Three boys and three girls were black; all the others were white.

Soon I stopped being just an observer, and began to interact with the children in situations where I couldn't avoid it. Fights often broke out when the teachers' backs were turned or they were busy far across the room. It was a big room, roughly fifty by thirty-five feet, and the high ceiling increased the noise level. With twenty-four children, it was hard always to see trouble start. Marilyn said she'd be glad if I would help a hurt child, or keep anyone from getting injured.

When I began as a junior high school teacher on the

Lower East Side in New York, and later in the East Bronx, there were three or four fights a day. Trying to hold children apart, I'd say something like "Why are you hurting each other?" or "Why do you want to hurt each other?" But these questions seemed to increase the intensity of the fighting. Finally I learned to say, "I *know* you don't want to hurt each other," or "You really *don't want* to hurt each other," and the fighting usually stopped. The truth was that I wasn't sure that they didn't want to hurt each other, or that human beings basically don't want to harm one another, but had learned pragmatically that saying this tended to stop the children from fighting. It was only much later that I realized that asking, "Why do you *want* to hurt each other?" —in other words, attributing volition to their behavior—merely increased their fear.

As I became more involved with the children, I remembered what Denah Harris had emphasized: "Try to find out what causes people to act *as though* they were evil." She asks people who work with her never to act on the basis of faith, either in her or in any theory. She asks them to act on a healthy skepticism until their own experiences in applying the theory lead to conviction based on the solution of problems. After all, that is the only basis for accepting the validity of any theory.

She is convinced, on the basis of many years of experience, that people don't want to hurt each other. My wife, Barbara, tended to agree with her but I wasn't convinced. But we both understood that the reason for telling children who were fighting that they didn't want to hurt each other was to relieve their fears that they *did.* They had been taught that they *wanted* to. I began working with Harris's basic assumption that people are *not* innately evil because I had already seen that children's fears *could* be unlearned, and that boys in junior high school had stopped fighting when their fears were relieved.

Though I knew only one technique to stop children from fighting, it was imperative to try it. Once or twice, I held back out of a sense of trying not to interfere, and a child got hurt. It was my responsibility as an adult to prevent this. I didn't step in at the first sign of conflict or disagreement, but if the children started to hurt each other, I did not hesitate to intervene. Gradually, I began to know the children better, to learn why they fought and how to help them not to fight but to relate as friends instead.

The Montessori Method seemed to me to hold back too much, overcompensating for the controlling pedagogies it was trying to replace. When two children fought on the playground, and one of them complained to the teacher, she usually said, "Go back and tell Arthur that you don't like to be hit," or "Tell Arthur I said not to do it." Though they tried, I rarely saw teachers intervene with any information that helped the children to resolve their differences. The teachers simply weren't taught to do this.

The Montessori Method didn't offer a theory, or practice, to help children not to fight, or to resolve their conflicts. Implicit in the theory seemed to be the idea that children could and would work it out themselves. They *would* have to learn to solve their own problems, without the constant intervention of adults. But people do only what they know how to do, and it became clear that the teachers didn't have the necessary information which would help the children deal with these conflicts.

I thought nursery school would be a place where children learned songs and games and numbers, and primarily how to live with each other. Apparently I forgot, or never knew, how much conflict, confusion, and pain a child experienced in a single day. Now, as some of the other teachers, began to invite me to observe in their classrooms, I saw virtually the same thing in all of them: threatening and fighting, boys against boys, boys against girls, girls against girls, taunting and conspiracies.

It's true, of course, that children must ultimately learn to solve their own problems, which they do by trial and error. But in this process, they primarily use information given to them by adults or they watch adults to see how they solve similar problems of conflict. Most children see adults call each other names, withdraw, threaten, and even strike. When they have differences, therefore, the children use these same techniques to try to settle them. Unless they get some new information, children act out these fight or flight ideas, and the problems don't get solved.

In any case, the children at my school fought often, particularly the boys. When they weren't fighting, they played war games, or cops and robbers. Most of their games, much of their interaction, involved the apparent conflict of interest between people, the battle between the good guys and the bad guys. There was a constant ordering and reordering of alliances and coalitions, first against one, then against another. A few children kept the same friends from day to day, and stayed out of the mainstream of the fighting and the arguing, but most of the boys and girls couldn't depend on each other's friendship. In their constant making and breaking of alliances, they seemed more like governments in world politics than children in nursery school.

In contrast, Denah Harris's theory emphasized that one of the normal functions of the human brain cortex is to solve problems, and that parents and teachers could help children organize their perceptions in a way that *sustains* the normal functioning of the cortex. A human brain uncrippled by moral theory, by a fearful obsession with death as a punishment for committing sins, could solve any human problem. The capabilities of the organism are virtually infinite; there are ways to solve problems we haven't yet begun to imagine, much less to learn. Harris asked me to observe the children, keeping in mind that their problematic behavior was a reflection of their attempts to think. This helped me to see that much of what they did or said was some form of question about the world they were learning to live in, which they acted out instead of asking in words.

I also began to meet weekly with parents to exchange information, since it would have been virtually impossible to explore these ideas without their help and cooperation. We discussed the questions the children raised, and the answers we were or were not giving them. For example, when the children asked questions in school about sex, and the physiology of reproduction, I tried to answer them accurately and thoroughly. A few parents didn't want me to discuss any aspect of physiology; I asked them to take the responsibility for telling their children not to listen to me when I discussed these topics with other children. How could I tell some children they couldn't listen to what I was saying, and others that they could? The parents who objected asked me to remind their children, if they asked questions, that their parents didn't want them to have this information, or, at least not from me.

This problem never emerged. Those parents made it clear to their children that they weren't to talk to me, or listen to me if I talked about reproduction, and the children obeyed. A few parents told their children not to listen to me at all, and they didn't. One child told me that her mother ordered her "not to listen to that mess," that it was against God's wishes for her to know about her body.

Religion was even more problematic than sex. The children asked many questions about God, which at first I tried to hedge or avoid. Later on, I tried to answer them, but some parents told their children not to ask me these questions. They said they didn't object to us discussing reproduction, or excretion, but if their children wanted to talk about religion, I should change the subject. Religion, these parents insisted, was an entirely personal matter. If I introduced the children to any ideas which differed with theirs, I undermined their authority. They asked me not to ask or answer any questions about God or religion.

I listened carefully when parents differed with me about their children. When we differed, we tried to convince each other. If they weren't convinced by what I said, I didn't insist on being right, since I felt that our interests were, ultimately, mutual. One aspect of my work was to support the children's relationships with their parents.

Little by little, the children began to approach me. I still sat in a small chair against the wall, watching and listening. They asked me to tie their shoes, to help them on with their coats, to hold their hands when we went to the playground. They wanted me to get things for them and to do things with them. They drew me in to the life of the class. If I was late to school, they asked for me and waited for me.

Some of the other teachers became friendly, pointing out things I could do to help, and day-to-day details about working with young children that I needed to know. They also let me know when I wasn't helpful—like when I went on talking to the children about fighting while Marilyn was trying to get them across the street to the playground.

They asked me what I noticed. What I thought of the school. And especially, what I thought of Marky—of the powerful effect he had on Marilyn's entire class, through his own fear and the fear he caused in the other children.

Marky was six when I met him, the biggest boy in the class. He was stocky, almost fat, and had brown hair and freckles across his nose. His walk was somewhere between a swagger and a waddle. When he was listening, which was hard for him to do, he squinted one eye and screwed up his nose. Marky never worked alone with a teacher, and rarely with another child. He was very alert, and liked to work with his hands. He liked anything mechanical. He took apart old clocks, and built things with lumber. We had a sawhorse, hammer, nails, and a saw in the classroom. Marky used them to build death machines—bombers, machine guns, torture devices, and robots which destroyed people.

He described himself as a robot. He said he wasn't a boy, that he had no brain or blood. He didn't like to be hugged, or even touched by anyone. When he was frightened or frustrated, Marky hit both children and teachers. He was strong and determined, and he hit hard. Some teachers tried to restrain him, but he was almost too strong for them to stop without actually fighting with him, so *they* stopped. They were afraid of him.

Marky learned to think of himself as a monster. His teachers and classmates eventually began to act toward him as if they agreed. They were afraid of Marky's sudden attacks. If Marky wanted a toy, he grabbed it, and he hit. At the same time, he refused to be separated from the class for any reason. He loved to build, but he refused to go alone to the lumberyard with me, for fear that a plot against him would develop in his absence. In the classroom he plotted constantly, and when he wasn't building war machines he was playing war games, monster games, or making "poison potions" with paint and soapy water.

Most of the children imitated Marky's games, his way of playing, his way of talking, and to a lesser extent, his way of relating. Denah Harris calls this kind of response "understudying"—the attempt to understand behavior, often frightening behavior, by imitating it.

One of the games Marky played was "Hot Pot." It was a variation of "Capture the Flag" or "Prisoner's Base"; a tag game in which the girls were "It." The object of the game was for the boys to capture the girls, to put them in a jail called the "Hot Pot," and after they were all captured, boil them alive.

Both boys and girls appeared to play this game with great pleasure and excitement. Their faces were flushed, and they shrieked as they ran. As I came to know the children, and watched more closely, I thought I saw signs of terror in their excitement; their bodies were rigid, their pulses throbbed, and their faces contorted. Yes, they seemed to be frightened, but when Marky instigated the game, they went along. When Marky wasn't in school, they also played this game, but less zealously.

Danny and Eddie formed a trio with Marky. They combined in every possible way, first Marky and Eddie against Danny, then Danny and Eddie against Marky, and so on. Both Danny and Eddie looked terrified most of the time, and their parents complained that the boys were afraid to go to school because of Marky. Other parents also complained about him, but no one knew what to do. When he was absent, the level of tension in the classroom went way down; when Marky was in school, it was as if he were a hunter and his classmates were his game.

Marky's parents were divorced. He lived with his mother, his grandmother, and his two-year-old sister. Before they were separated, his father beat his mother, sometimes in front of Marky. His father resented the children, and often beat Marky when he came to visit. We learned this much later, toward the end of the school year, when Marilyn and I had dinner with Marky's mother. Though she often spanked him, she was afraid of Marky, too. Earlier, Marilyn often tried to make appointments with Mrs. Stein, but without success.

I'd like to say that I helped Marky to solve his problems, but I didn't. What I was able to do was too little and too late. I told him that he wasn't a monster, that his father didn't really want to hurt him or his mother, and that his mother didn't want to hurt him either. He listened, but he didn't believe me. His mother withdrew from all attempts to reach Marilyn, except for the one dinner we had together. On the basis of that meeting, which was friendly and open, we could have begun to work together to help Marky, but it was already the end of the year.

Though Marky may not have learned much from me, I

learned a lot from him. I learned the overwhelming effect that fear can have on a child who has been repeatedly punished, and the effect that such a frightened child can have on all the children around him.

Marky wasn't the "rotten apple" which spoils the barrel. His fear was infectious, but he wasn't rotten in any sense. He, too, came out of a much larger barrel—the world. Every class I subsequently worked in or visited had many children who acted out the same problems Marky did, in the same way, although most of the time their fears were less obvious and tormenting.

From Marky I learned that children act out their questions about things they see, hear, and experience which frighten them. Although I didn't know enough then to answer Marky's questions, my ability to hear them improved and I began to see more and more of the other children's behavior as questions for which they needed answers.

Fortunately, the children increasingly began to see me as a friend. One child referred to me as the "Help Department." Another told me I was her friend because "You talk about real things"; I was, she told her mother, "the oldest boy in the class."

2

Fear Is a Four-Letter Word

A friend of mine, Lou, was in a restaurant with his three-and-a-half-year-old son when the lights suddenly went out. The boy groped in the dark for his father's hand, finally reached it and squeezed it hard.

"Are you afraid, Ned?" my friend asked.

"I'm not afraid, Daddy."

"It's all right to be afraid, Ned."

"I'm afraid, Daddy."

Lou had helped his child to talk about fear. He welcomed the opportunity which is often forbidden and denied to children by parents, peers, and teachers. The exchange with his son led to a discussion of why people are afraid of the dark. Some parents think that discussing fear with children is projecting, putting ideas in a child's head. "You shouldn't even ask children if they're afraid," they say, much less tell them it's all right to be afraid. Why encourage them to become preoccupied with something they wouldn't otherwise think about? I found, though, that discussing fear with children seemed to diminish it, once they could bring themselves to talk about it.

At first, the children at my nursery school usually denied

that they were afraid of anything. For example, they said they were not afraid of the monsters, witches, and ghosts they saw on television, in cartoons, old movies, and children's programs. They had already learned that it was "bad" to be afraid. Frequently, when they fell down in the playground, they would bounce up quickly, brave smiles fixed and frozen on their faces. "I'm not afraid, I'm not afraid!" they said, denying the accusation that no one had made. Since infancy, they'd learned to deny fear; they knew they were supposed to be brave little boys and girls who weren't scared of anything.

As we sat around the work table together, drawing and reading, I occasionally raised questions about fear with them. "Are you afraid of spanking, of Mommy or Daddy getting angry, of robbers?" I asked. Even though they were beginning to know me, the answer was still "No, we're not afraid of anything." I soon learned that children wouldn't talk openly about their fears in groups, but they would talk about them alone with me. Inevitably, many of these fears were ultimately related to the fear of death.

Eve Lazar, a friend who is a clinical psychologist, also found that children denied having any fears when asked directly. She began to ask them if they knew of any fears their friends had; suddenly all kinds of answers poured out. When I tried this, there were similar results:

"My friend is afraid of ghosts."

"My friend is afraid of being drafted [the "friend" was six years old]."

"My friend is afraid of monsters."

"My friend is afraid that fish will kill him when he swims."

"I know this kid who is afraid to sleep with the light off!"

"I know this kid who is afraid his daddy will beat up his mommy. Maybe he'll kill her!"

They were talking about themselves.

Some children's fears were most intense, and clearly on the surface, like Terry's. He was a five-year-old boy who constantly acted out his anxious questions about death; a bright, big-eyed, curly-haired child who panicked easily. His father moved out of the house after Terry's birth, and denied that Terry was his child. Terry was confused, upset, and frightened about why his father wouldn't talk to him, even when they passed each other on the street, but he never spoke about it.

Terry's mother read him Bible stories at bedtime. He was fascinated with the story of the Crucifixion. On our daily walk to the playground, the class passed a five-and-ten-cent store that displayed pictures of Christ on the cross, and Terry always stopped to look.

Much of Terry's time was given over to fantasy. He would make paper cutouts of television superheroes and monsters and fly them around the room. He announced that he was Gigantor, or Batman, or Dracula, and told long violent stories about his adventures. It was hard for him to concentrate on putting on his shoes, getting dressed to go outside, or even sitting down to have juice and cookies.

To me, he seemed preoccupied with questions about the TV programs he was watching and the Bible stories he heard, but the teachers were too busy to hear them. After all, they were responsible for twenty-three children, and Terry was very trying. He was also severely troubled, very unhappy, unable to cooperate with the school's program because he was so obsessed with questions that no one answered or even acknowledged. He couldn't formulate them in words, but what he wanted to ask was something like: "Why won't my father talk to me? Is it because I did something wrong? Am I bad? Why did they crucify Jesus?" and "Why do monsters and superheroes fight and punish people all the time?"

Later, he raised these questions with me and with his

mother. The other children in the class watched the same television programs, heard some of the same Bible stories, and had many of the same questions, but Terry was more desperate. Children often won't talk in school about problems, or troubling events which happen at home, because they're not encouraged to, but Terry did. Most teachers don't think that discussing these problems with children is their function. Some schools have a staff psychologist to whom they refer the more obviously troubled children; in such cases problems are usually seen as pathological questions for trained authorities, not for teachers. But if teachers don't learn to answer children's painful and troubling questions about life in and outside of their homes, how can these troubled children be free to concentrate on learning? How can they think about reading and writing, when they are so confused and fearful?

One day, Terry told me that a man tried to shoot him with a shotgun, while he was on his way to school. The man had been sitting high up in an apartment house window. "I could tell from the look in his eyes," Terry said. "He was going to shoot me, but I think he was scared of me. He had a motorcycle in the garage."

I asked Terry if he had ever seen anything like this on television, or in the movies, or heard anyone discuss it. Was this a dream? Both children and adults sometimes find that dreams and reality overlap. Late in the day we realize that something we thought we lived, we've only dreamed.

TERRY: No, none of those things. I saw it in real life.

ME: How could you see his eyes from so far away?

TERRY: I have magic vision.

ME: I think you heard that story somewhere.

TERRY: I did not!

ME: But why would a man shoot you?

TERRY: Because he's a kidnapper. He shoots children, and when they die, he puts on a disguise like a good guy. He was going to shoot me!

ME: That's pretty frightening.

TERRY: Yeah. I saw him, and he saw me. I saw him beginning to shoot me.

ME: What made him stop?

TERRY: I made a bird call, like this: "*whooosh.*" A pigeon came over and gave him a message. You know what it said? "This is the devil. You will come to Hell at midnight, and you will die. Ho, ho, ho."

ME: Have you been thinking about dying lately?

TERRY: No, no [trying to laugh, but not managing it]. The message said to tell the man who was trying to kill me, ha, ha, ha. . . . He worked for the devil.

ME: Do you ever think about dying or getting killed?

TERRY: No! [frightened] No, no, no!

ME: But you thought this man was going to kill you . . . ?

TERRY (*softly*): Right.

ME (*gently*): You know, if you are thinking about death, I can try to answer some of your questions.

TERRY: I think about it a lot.

But before I could begin to talk to Terry about death, he went on to tell a joke about worms eating people, and insisted that Dracula put "X" marks on corpses. These statements themselves represented a willingness to raise questions about death. Once children realize that you will try to give straight answers, they flood you with all the questions they have been saving up, that no one has answered for them before. Often they don't even wait for your response, but go on pouring out question after question, as if to say, "Will you answer this one? And this one? And is it all right to talk about this?" They are so relieved that they can bring up these subjects, which have previously been taboo, that for a while the answer becomes secondary to the relief they feel about not being punished or shamed for asking the questions.

The effect of these obsessional ideas on Terry was devastating. He told me many stories, for example, about threats to his life. I tried to help him articulate the questions, when I heard them, but often I didn't understand the questions within his stories, because I didn't know enough about his life outside of school. War games, wild animals, monsters, robbers—he was acting out his questions, desperately looking for help in coping with fears about death that society had taught him.

One day Terry walked around the room, humming to himself. Finally he muttered, "When I tell people, 'Some day I'm going to be dead,' they say, 'Now look, kid, stop making jokes. I know you won't die.' "You see?" he continued, "I *can't* tell anyone what I think about dying, because no one will listen to me!"

If what Terry said was true, why wouldn't anyone listen? Why couldn't anyone listen? Terry said that when he told his mother about his fears of death, she told him not to talk silly. He didn't know it, of course, but by telling her, he raised her fears for him and for herself. She lived alone with him, and worried about the street crime in their neighborhood. She tried to reassure herself and Terry by telling him that his fears were unfounded—but they weren't. They were exaggerated but based on reality.

When Terry told his teachers about these fears, he raised their own unresolved and largely repressed anxieties about death, and their fear of his effect on the other children. The teachers were not unresponsive; they knew his fears were important, but they had been taught like most of us, not to think about death—it was taboo. Like Terry, they had learned that thinking about death would make them ill, make them crazy, or even make them dead. They didn't want to encourage his worrying; besides, he was "a morbid child," bright, but somewhat "disturbed." They ignored his questions and fantasies, or tried to divert him to less violent games or to "work." They could answer questions about language and numbers, but not about the taboo subjects he raised. But his questions and fantasies were his most imperative work—work he had to do before he could fully concentrate on traditional school subjects. It was important and helpful that the teachers shifted Terry's focus gently from fantasy to reality, but they weren't able to ascribe any importance to the dreams, fears, and fantasies which were real to him.

The result of such a response to a child like Terry is that either his obsessional fears will be repressed in the process of living and growing, so that he will develop defenses against thinking about them (as most of us do), or, without the information he needs as a response to his questions, he will continue to be obsessed, and perhaps act these questions out as an adolescent, beginning a tragic new stage.

Other children often told me stories like Terry's. They usually made clearer distinctions between what they saw and what really happened to them, but not always. If children are given the chance, their questions about what they've seen and heard in all areas, particularly death and violence, will pour out, often as stories or games. *It is because children are not taught any effective language for asking taboo questions that they act these questions out.*

Terry groped with the idea that we are all judged for our sins, as to whether we shall live or die. He learned this from our culture: The good guys live and the bad guys die. Since the latter are punished with death, it is important to be a good guy, and one way we can recognize the good guys is that they punish the bad guys.

Terry had learned not that death is a biological and chemical finality, but that it is the ultimate punishment for being bad. He learned this from the Bible stories his mother read him, from the television shows he watched—Perry Mason as will as *Horror Theatre*—and saw that this ritualized punishment is carried out in the real world as well.

Children need to be sure that commonplace activities do not hide a threat to their lives. A walk in the country may mean bee stings to a city child, who wants to know if bee stings can kill him.

"My friend is afraid that fish will kill him if he swims," a little girl told me.

"Do you know why?" I asked her.

"He saw this movie where this man gets eaten by a shark."

I explained to her that sharks sometimes did kill and eat people, and that was terrible, but that millions of people swam millions of times without it ever happening to them. The chances of it happening to her were small.

Unfortunately, five-year-olds care little about probability theory. Their world is smaller than ours, and possibilities seem more limited to them. Since most of them only know a few people, and are familiar with relatively few places, in their minds the chances of a shark's biting them are pretty good. My answer may not have relieved this girl's fear completely, but probably helped reduce it.

I also explained to her that someone who was killed by a shark would immediately stop feeling pain; she would go into shock and thus would not experience being eaten. I then tried to make clear what shock was. At death, I concluded, the person's brain would stop working, she would then no longer be alive, and she would stop feeling or experiencing anything. Death would be an end to this pain, not a beginning.

Children often raised questions about the threat of death from wolves. They had learned through folk tales like *Little Red Riding Hood,* through comics, and possibly *Peter and the Wolf,* that wolves frequently attack and kill people. According to naturalist Farley Mowat, however, who observed Arctic wolves for years, Arctic wolves *don't* kill people; in fact, they feed mainly on field mice and an occasional old reindeer, when they can catch one. Mowat observed the wolves, they observed him, and there was no attack from either side. I told the children that this expert on the lives of wolves was unable to find any evidence that Arctic wolves had ever killed anyone in the Canadian Northwest or Alaska. They were very relieved to hear this, and so was I.

We are all very aware that there are many frightening things in this world. I never told the children that there was *nothing* to fear, or that all fear was irrational. I answered their questions about animal and human violence in order to put their fears into perspective, to distinguish between the real and the unreal, the likely and the unlikely: When a fear had a basis in reality, I tried to give as much information about the phenomenon as possible. When I knew little or nothing about the questions the children raised, I tried to get the information for them, or at least to tell them where to get it, knowing even that would help somewhat to relieve their fears. Above all, I emphasized the necessity of using their innate ability to get information wherever they could, continuing to ask questions of everyone, and using their brains to solve problems.

I urged the children to ask their relatives and their friends' parents for information, if their parents and teachers couldn't answer their questions. Many of these children could already read. They might eventually find the answers to their questions in books. If they couldn't immediately find them, I told them, they would some day be able to develop solutions to problems as yet unsolved.

But as we all know, there are questions and there are questions: some are dangerous to ask, and some of the most frightening and puzzling "entertainments" in children's lives are cartoons and films about the "undead" and monsters, where questions about the nature of death arise.

Horror and monster films like *Bride of Frankenstein* and *The Devil Commands* attempt to explore the question of death as a punishment. They often end with the warning that Man can't know, is not supposed to know, the meaning of the mysteries of life and death. Traditionally, in the horror film, the mad scientist attempts to play God—to create life from a corpse, or pieces of corpses. This is the Frankenstein myth, as well as the myth of the Golem from Hebrew mythology, that life—consciousness—can be created from the remains of life or from death.

The scientist succeeds in creating a monster, usually a grotesque, mindless, will-less creature, who at first carries out his creator's wishes, but then develops its own will. Often the monster requires the blood of living victims to keep itself "alive." It soon goes berserk, killing, rampaging, and destroying.

Sometimes poetic justice is meted out, when the monster turns on the scientist and kills him. In another variation, the scientist destroys the monster, or himself and the monster, at the end of the film. Often the mad scientist's laboratory explodes, usually destroyed by a terrific charge of lightning. As the laboratory burns, remember the sepulchral, somber voice, off-screen and other-worldly, explaining that there are some secrets Man may never know. The implication is that death and destruction, presumably by a wrathful God, is punishment for man's presumption in trying to create life, in trying to possess forbidden knowledge. These films continue that part of the myth of the Garden of Eden which forbids Adam and Eve (and all human beings) to eat from the tree of the knowledge of good and evil. It rewards passivity and punishes curiosity with banishment or death; only an evil man dares do this work of God's, and death is his punishment.

At least horror films *attempt* to deal with punishment, death, and retribution. So do Saturday morning cartoons. That's why so many children find them fascinating, and prefer them to the "educational" programs parents choose for them. Though horror movies and violent cartoons don't provide children with any helpful information, and indeed frighten them with their misinformation, children are fascinated with them because they deal with the taboo topic children are most interested in: death, as a punishment for being bad.

Children often have nightmares after watching these programs, but many watch them whenever they can. Adults, seeing the children spellbound, identify this fascination as "liking." Thus children learn to identify their sensation of horrified fascination as pleasure, just as we did when we were young. Do you remember being told that you liked to be scared, that you liked ghost stories and the thrill of the supernatural? We learned to enjoy feeling scared as long as there was no real danger. Listening to ghost stories, reading *Tales from the Crypt*, watching *Dracula*, we experienced the thrill of mock danger, knowing we were safe.

We denied a threat of death, which we "knew" wasn't real for us—but in fact it was. We were taught to be obsessed with death as a punishment for not conforming, for daring to think, for asking questions, and for not obeying the authorities; in short, we were taught death is a punishment for being bad.

Children don't like horror stories any more than we like looking at the results of automobile accidents. We are drawn to them by what is called "morbid curiosity"; but it is really the fearful subject that fascinates, the need to learn what death is, and isn't, and whether or not it is a punishment for our "sins."

Both parents and children are maleducated to think they enjoy being frightened. One blowy winter morning, I boarded the crosstown bus after doing some Christmas shopping. Department store Santa Clauses rang their bells, hunched against the wind, and smoke puffed from their mouths and noses when they ho-ho'd. I sat down next to a boy who looked about six and a half, and his mother; they were deep in conversation:

BOY: For Christmas, I want a skeleton, locked up in a dungeon. It's a toy.

MOTHER: That sounds horrible! [pause] But . . . I suppose horror toys are supposed to be horrible.

BOY: I thought you *liked* horror movies.

MOTHER (*righteously*): Not *all* horror movies. Only the good ones!

That ended the conversation. The boy looked at his mother. She looked out of the window at the cold December streets. Then both of them, their faces set, turned and looked straight ahead.

3

Working with Parents

At the beginning of the school year, I wrote a short article for the parents' association newsletter, describing the research I hoped to do with the children, and asking interested parents to work with me.

A few months later, to follow up, I sent the following letter home with the children, and mailed duplicates, in case the notes fell off the safety pins which secured them to the children's coats:

> Dear Parents,
>
> I hope you and your family have a very happy New Year. I'm writing to ask for your help. As you know, I've been working with your child in Marilyn Benetti's class since September. I've been trying to learn the cause and extent of children's fear, and how this fear affects their ability to learn and to live. I've found, sadly, that many children are often afraid of discussing things they are unable to talk to adults about—usually the adults close to them. Here are some of their questions:
>
> "Are there monsters?"
>
> "Why do people get locked in jail?"
>
> "Why are some words 'bad' words?" "What do 'bad' words mean?"

"Why do my parents spank me if they love me?"

"How can I stop other children from hitting me? What can I say to them?"

"How does my body work?" "Why can't you talk about going to the toilet?"

"Is there a God?" "What is God like?" "Does He see everything I do?"

"What is death like? What will happen to me and my parents when we die?"

These are all most important questions, which I've been trying to answer in school, but I need your help. I'd like to work together with as many of you who can come, to meet regularly to help answer your children's questions, and help them to solve their problems.

Please call me at the school, or drop by any day after class to arrange the most convenient time and evening.

Yours for problem-solving.
Warm Regards.

Ten parents responded, and we agreed to have the first meeting at the Sterns' house. The Sterns were Evelyn's parents. After Evelyn got over the excitement of having her teacher in her house, and finished showing me all her toys and dolls, we were ready to begin.

Sitting around the small living room with me, on chairs and on the floor, were Mr. and Mrs. Stern, Mrs. Gaddis, Mrs. Johnson, Mr. and Mrs. Fineholtz, Mr. and Mrs. Gardner, Mrs. Shea, and Mrs. Weiner.

We sat, balancing coffee cups and wineglasses on our knees, waiting for Evelyn to go to bed. Finally, Mrs. Stern had a muffled talk with her in her room; a few words like "or else," and "no television" filtered through the closed door, there was sudden silence, and I began.

"For the last year and a half, I've been exploring the hypothesis that most young children are frightened most of the time, and that this fear blocks their ability to learn, to develop, and to make and sustain friendships with each other.

This fear prevents them from functioning in the way the innate design of their brains suggests that they can. It causes them to be in a state of pain and anxiety much of the time. I've been a teacher for ten years, and over and over again, I've seen irrational fear, threats, and punishment prevent learning.

"One of the main reasons I came to work in a nursery school was to learn through experience where my own fears developed. I chose to work with four- and five-year-olds because they are old enough to be articulate, and young enough not to have developed strong defenses and denial against fear.

"I've developed some techniques for dealing with the children's questions and problems, based on my exploration of social worker Denah Harris's theory of learning and human nature. The techniques are based on the premise that there are no good or bad children, no good or bad behavior. If people are born potentially perfect problem-solvers, then they can solve all reality problems. If they're not solving these problems, it's due to the misuse of their physiological equipment—their brains.

"If this is so, punishment won't help anyone to use their innate physiological potential more effectively. I don't punish because I don't think punishment ever solves any problems. It sometimes appears to solve problems for parents, but it ultimately creates more severe problems than it solves. I'm speaking of all punishment, not just corporal punishment. Any threat, any sanction, is a punishment. Whether it's the threat of removal of privileges, or temporary banishment, or the withdrawal of affection, any words or action that imply that stronger sanctions are on the way is punishment.

"I'm not saying I never act in a punishing or threatening way. I do, but not because I think it's a good idea or that it works. I yell at my wife sometimes, or at children, or at other drivers on the road, not because it helps any situation, but because I'm conditioned by my experience to yell, having been yelled at and seen others yell, and because I often don't know what else to do. I don't really mean I don't know what else to do, but that I haven't reprogrammed my thinking to be able to problem-solve automatically, instead of yelling automatically. Yelling, which is often interpreted and meant as a form of punishment, seems to make people so defensive that it prevents progress in solving problems, in a group or just between two people.

"I have punished children. Not very often, and *not* because I think they needed it, or I need to do it, but because I was punished as a child, and learned that that's what children need when they are bad. I think, though, that it's a mistake; it's disfunctional to yell; it doesn't solve problems. I'm trying to learn how not to do it. I don't think we should be embarrassed about making mistakes. I tell the children we learn by making mistakes, and it's true for us as well. Of course, you may not think that punishing or yelling at children is a mistake. Let's discuss that . . ."

MRS. STERN: What do you do with a child who hits?

ME: Whom does the child hit?

MRS. STERN: Well, I'm not necessarily talking about my child. He hits, but so do the other children in his class.

ME: Whom does he hit?

MRS. STERN: Almost everyone. [laughter] Me, his teacher, his classmates, his babysitter . . .

ME: A child learns to hit from seeing other people do it, and it's his way of asking why people hit. I try to answer the question I perceive in hitting. Of course, hitting him back or punishing him would be an answer, too, but not a helpful one.

MRS. STERN: It helps me [laughter].

ME: It seems to, for the moment, but doesn't the same situation and the same problem arise repeatedly?

MRS. STERN: Yes.

ME: Tell me what you do in a situation which you think calls for punishment. I'll tell you what I do, and we can get some consensus.

MRS. STERN: I told you, I hit. Or I say, "No television for a week."

MR. FINEHOLTZ: I don't think you should threaten children.

MRS. STERN: I don't think so either, unless you back it up.

MR. FINEHOLTZ: I don't think you should threaten or back it up. [turning to me] Are you saying that children are trying to cope with problems they face, when they hit or act difficult, and that punishment doesn't help them, it prevents them from solving problems?

ME: Yes, but I'd go a step further. Not only does punishment impede their ability to cope or solve problems, it can cripple it. They become focused on the punishment, instead of the solution to the problem.

MRS. FINEHOLTZ: But in trying to cope with life, the child has to explore certain alternatives in every case. Unless a child is restrained, or at least watched, he can hurt himself or another child. What do you do about that?

ME: I try to be alert, to keep children from hurting themselves or each other, if I can. It's also *how* you stop them that's important. You try to do it in a way that doesn't give them the idea that they're bad for exploring, for doing what they're doing. You stop them from acting in a destructive or hurtful way, but if they hurt someone or break something, I tell them they're not being destructive because they *want* to be. If you tell them they intend to be destructive, you're helping to perpetuate the destructive behavior by reinforcing the idea in the child's mind that he's bad. That's not the answer he needs.

MRS. GADDIS: What if the child hits you?

ME: If the child hits me, I think he's asking if I'll punish him if he's bad, and why other people punish him when he's bad, and why people hit each other. I gently hold him away if he's still hitting, and then I answer those questions, which I perceive in his behavior, rather than punishing him for punishing me. Human beings have been doing that for thousands of years, and it doesn't solve the problem.

MRS. STERN: Isn't he also asking if he can destroy you with his hitting? If he's angry, and he's allowed to hit, isn't one of his questions, "Is my anger going to kill or destroy you?"

ME: I think it's more likely that he's asking why people hit each other and why you'll hit him! I know the premise that the child is afraid that his anger will be so devastating it will destroy his parents if he gives into it. I think that's an inaccurate Freudian hypothesis. I don't think there's any physiological or empirical evidence to support that theory. It's also cynical and pessimistic; "we can't solve our problems, we are innately, competitively destructive. At best, we can only hope to adjust."

Mr. Gardner had been silent up to now, but he appeared more and more agitated. He seemed as if he were struggling to contain himself, but he finally burst out. "I don't hear any scientific evidence to support *your* theory, either! Who are you to question Freud's theories! I think it's pretty damn presumptuous! What the hell are your credentials?"

There was a shocked silence. "Can I get anyone more wine?" Mrs. Stern blushed. She began to move around the room, collecting empty glasses.

I felt attacked, but Mr. Gardner was very threatened. He was breathing fast, and his face was red.

"Mr. Gardner," I began, "I'm exploring a theory. It isn't mine, it was developed by Denah Harris, as I said earlier. I'm learning a theory of human nature which she's developed in clinical practice, over the past twenty-five years. I'm exploring a part of her theory which is helping me to understand why children are so frightened. I'm not a theoretician yet, though I have the potential to develop new theories, just as you and everyone else has that potential. There *is* scientific evidence to support Harris's theories about the physiology of brain function, and she's applying what is known about brain function to explain human behavior. All I'm asking you to do is evaluate these ideas for yourself. I explored the ideas and my conclusions are based on my experience. Harris has many years of clinical experience and data, which do demonstrate the solution of many problems Freudian theory states are unsolvable. You can reach your own conclusions about this theory by testing it for yourself.

"You asked about my credentials; I have just a B.A. and the urgent need to solve problems. As for questioning Freud's theories, any theory is open to question by anyone. More important, the test of a theory is whether or not it accurately describes reality or solves a problem. What do you think?"

MR. GARDNER (*less angrily*): I don't know . . .

MRS. JOHNSON: Since we're raising those kinds of questions, why do you keep saying, "*He* did this, *he* did that"? Why don't you ever say "she"? Don't "she's" do anything?

ME: I'm sorry. You're right. There's no word except "the child," or "the children" which covers both boys and girls at the same time. I'll try to remember to say "she."

MRS. GARDNER: How can you socialize people if you don't disapprove of them for antisocial acts—make them feel bad in some way for doing bad? It seems to me, that's an answer to the question, "If I do wrong, will I be disapproved of?" The answer is *yes*, so don't do it; and that's reality!

ME: I don't think you'd want to give that answer to your children, would you? Society will do it without you. Why add to your children's pain and maleducation? There's no valid reason I can think of to use superior force, or to make anyone believe he or she is bad. It *is* true that if they act in ways that society calls bad, they'll be punished. Your children will get plenty of reinforcement for the idea that they're bad, from society, without your help. But I think we need to redefine these concepts of good and bad. Children and adults often act destructively, but are they "bad" for doing it? What are we actually seeing in this behavior we've learned to call bad? Isn't problematic behavior the result of thinking, and "badness" a learned idea about behavior?

Because I don't think people are good and bad, I don't punish but I also don't praise children, because I don't want to condition behaviorism. We shouldn't train children, we should educate them; training is for dogs and horses. I'll tell a child, "That was very helpful," or "That was very thoughtful," instead of "That was nice" or "That was good." I'll say, if I see her act destructively, "That wasn't thoughtful" or "That was destructive," or "That hurt! Get off my toe!"

I try not to use "destructive" too often, because it might be closely associated with "bad" in her mind. I know it's awkward, and I have to search for words, but I don't want to maleducate the child to the idea that she's good if she's done this, and bad if she's done that.

The critical difference between this approach and the moral one is that I don't punish the children or withdraw my affection if they act destructively, and I don't base my empathy for them on their constructive behavior, or their conformity to my ideas. Or at least, I try hard not to. I'm trying not to use words that children interpret as judgmental, because this hurts them, and stops their progress. At the same time, I tell them that you *can* use words to tell people how their actions affect you. I watch them and listen to them, to perceive the questions they're acting out. When I'm perceptive, it works! When I'm not, all I can do is tell the children they've hurt me, but sometimes, it doesn't seem to make a damn bit of difference. A child bit and kicked me the other day, and I felt like I was going to go right off the ground.

MRS. SHEA: Well, I find that children solve problems better when there are no adults around. They seem to do it without fighting.

ME: That hasn't been my experience. It depends on what information and experience the children have. They're likely to do whatever they've seen other children do, or what their parents and the culture they live in have told them to do. There are quite a few children in this school whose parents tell them to hit anyone who bothers them, because the culture teaches the parents that is what is "right" to do. That doesn't solve the problem. I'm saying that children can't resolve their differences without accurate information from adults. I'm trying to help them to solve the problems the adult world has failed to solve. Fight or flight . . . or stand still in terror. That's what the adult world teaches them.

MRS. SHEA: What do you say or do with a child who hits you?

ME: Mrs. Stern asked me that earlier; so let's take an example: The other day, a child named Terry jumped on me from the top of some shelves. The impact knocked me off a radiator I'd been sitting on, on to the floor. I'd asked him repeatedly to let me finish talking to another child, and he got impatient. As I fell off the radiator, I burned my arm on a pipe connected to it. Terry also hit me in the nose, inadvertently, as part of his jump.

I started to yell at him. All I said was that he hurt me. I didn't say he was bad, or that I'd punish him, but he started to cry. He's particularly frightened of being yelled at. Most of the children think about violence, and talk about it most of the time. Terry talks about violence all the time.

He was shocked that I'd yelled at him. He ran into the book corner and threw himself down on the mat. After a few moments, I went over to him and said, "Look, I panicked. I wasn't thinking when I yelled at you. I didn't do it because I wanted to, or because I thought you needed it. I know you didn't mean to hurt me, but I just got frightened, and did what I learned adults do when I was a child like you. I'm sorry, my brain wasn't working very well, but you really hurt and scared me.

"You scared me, too," he said, sniffling.

"I know I did," I said. "I'll try not to do it again."

He knew what I meant when I said my brain wasn't working very well, because I'd taught him some elementary brain physiology, and some general physiology. That's a large part of what I'm doing. Some of the first questions children ask are "Who am I?" "What am I?" and "How do I work?" From pulling things off shelves when they're very tiny, to playing with their feces, to hurting bugs or animals or other people, to taking things apart, to rolling off the bed when they are very small, most of their behavior is an attempt to get this information.

Buckminster Fuller said children are perfect scientists. A child throws a toy out of a crib, or drops a spoon from his high chair, over, and over. Though it exasperates parents, the child is experimenting with gravity, and he learns something each time. Fuller said a baby who turns over on her back or stomach is making great discoveries for herself about the laws of gravity. She's learning about the relationship of her own mass to the mass of the earth.

Everything a child does from the moment it leaves the uterus (some say before) indicates that his or her brain is working to solve problems; that it's instinctively trying to order millions of sensory impressions. When children learn language, like your children, they ask questions about how the world works, and their relationship to it. They want to know what will happen, and why, if they express or act out ideas which they've learned are problematic. They want to know about cause and effect. I try to get them to verbalize the questions they act out; "What is it you're asking me?" "Can you say the question in words?"

If a child cries, and has difficulty talking, I say, very gently, "Tell me in words what happened, or what you want, and I'll try to help you. If you can just stop crying long enough to do that, I can hear you and begin to help. I know you feel sad and frightened."

It's important to acknowledge children's worry, fear, and hurt, because it's relieving for them. Often, but not always, that will stop a child from crying, if she's convinced you mean it. Sometimes when a child is having a tantrum, saying "I know you feel frightened" will help cut into it. What happens in a tantrum is that a circuit in the brain keeps replaying over and over, without the child's being able to think or evaluate what he or she is doing. It's the unconscious playback of some terrifying past event or circumstance which hasn't been understood or evaluated. If you gently ask the child to tell you what he was thinking while he was having the tantrum, and he *is* able to recall it, you can help him to evaluate the memory; evaluate it together, and you've taken the first step in breaking up this painful, unevaluated ritual, and relieving the child and yourself of a great deal of unnecessary pain.

During a tantrum, a child is out of touch with current reality, reliving memories, but one can help the child back. It's a mistake to deliberately let a child cry out a tantrum because that reinforces the child's fear that no one cares. Children think that we know everything. If we don't try to help them when they are so desperate, and don't hear their questions, they think we don't care. They don't realize it's not because we're unwilling to help, but because we often don't know how.

We don't know how to do many of the things we need to do; we haven't been taught to carry out these functions of parent, husband, wife, friend, or child. We have had to learn what we know the hard way, but if we knew how, we could make it easier for our children to become parents, and take pleasure in helping their own children.

MR. STERN: Is punishment always so destructive?

ME: About the least negative result of punishment is that the solution of the problem will be postponed rather than prevented. We punish because somewhere, somehow, we were taught to punish and were punished ourselves. Most of us punish children because we don't know how to solve the problems that we're punishing them for. We all do the best we know how, though. If we knew how to do more, or better, we would. We all can make choices if we perceive options—not between good and evil, which are opposite sides of the same moral coin, but between thinking and behavior that demonstrably solve the problems of living, and thinking and behavior that don't.

There isn't one "right" way, as opposed to the wrong way, or the one "true" way, as opposed to the false ways. The values underlying the Harris theory and approach require the search for solutions which are constructive to all, and destructive to none. Not "the greatest good for the greatest number of people," but a rational, cooperative life for all human beings. We're rapidly reaching a point in world history where everyone's needs will be met, or no one's will.

MRS. SHEA: That's fine, but sometimes I just can't take it any more. My children keep hitting each other, and I keep asking them to stop. Finally, I'm exhausted. I sock them. It's not my style to withdraw, so I hit them to make them stop.

ME: I know how you feel, but don't you see how irrational that is? You're hitting someone to teach him not to hit someone else.

MRS. SHEA: I don't care, really, as long as they stop doing it. When they don't hit each other, they use words like "dodo head," and "fuckhead" to each other. I think the basic hostility between siblings is inevitable, even though they have their good moments, sometimes. When you introduce a new sibling into a child's life, you introduce a conflict that he'll have to cope with the rest of his life, and never successfully resolve. I know that's fatalistic, but I believe it.

ME: Most people would agree with you, but I'm exploring alternatives to that theory. From what I've begun to learn, I don't think it's accurate. If you agree with the theory of sibling rivalry, you need to know that it's a theory, not a fact, just like what I'm saying about not punishing children is a theory. We see children hit each other, and hear various interpretations as to why they do it. One of them is that sibling rivalry is an innate phenomenon, that it has to happen in a family with more than one child. I don't agree, because I've seen families where it doesn't happen. And where it does happen, I can usually find out where and how the children learned that they were expected to be jealous of the baby.

I don't think intra-species violence is innate in human beings, because I know of at least two tribes, numbering thousands of members, who have no history of violence, going back hundreds, maybe thousands of years. One tribe is the Temiar of Malaya, and the other is the Pygmies. They have no history of suicide, no mental illness, no murder, and no jails.

MRS. SHEA: But don't they have their own outlets for violence that we would consider strange? Maybe they're violent in other ways.

ME: Well, they don't go around killing each other, and they don't make war, which raises not only the question of who or what is normal for human beings, but what is primitive behavior?

MRS. WEINER: I think I'm with Mrs. Shea—about hitting kids, that is. After twelve hours of being with my kids, I've had it. They know I'm not going to leave them, because what I do is stay around and yell. They become too much for me, and I have to hit them.

ME: After four hours of being with twenty-two five- and

six-year olds, I've had it, too. But of course, I can go home. You're already home, so what can you do? You don't enjoy yelling at them, I know. Wouldn't you like to have an alternative response? Does that sound like a leading question? [laughter]

MRS. WEINER: I'm just not sure that anything else I could do wouldn't convey the same sense of exasperation.

ME: Wouldn't you rather convey the expectation that they don't have to relate to each other that way?

MRS. WEINER: I don't believe it!

ME: Maybe you don't believe it, but I think you'd like to. Let me share with you some of the techniques I tried. If they make sense, you can try them. I'll just tell you my experiences. I would ask your son, "Where did you see that kind of hitting? Who did it?"

The children call each other "nigger" and "motherfucker," and I ask them where they heard those words, and they tell me. Then I try to explain to them, or figure out with them, why the person they saw hitting, or heard cursing, is doing that. Sometimes, if it's a classmate they're speaking about, I say, "Come on, let's go ask her, or him."

A lot of the name calling comes from children's television, like "dummy," and "dodo." It's sad that children learn to think of themselves and others as dumb or stupid, on "educational" programs. In answer to this, I tell the children that no one is stupid. Everyone is born with a brain he or she can learn to use to solve problems if he is allowed to, and not called bad, dumb, or stupid for acting out questions about anything he hears, sees, or experiences. No one is stupid.

MRS. STERN: Do they understand what stupid means?

ME: Yes. Stupid means bad to them; it's a synonym for inferior. It's a category you put other people in, and try to avoid getting put into yourself, because it's a way of being "deaded." "Deaded" is different from "killed." It's Harris's concept for relating to a human being as if he had no needs; not to kill him, but to treat him as if he were dead; *to symbolically bury him alive*. When a marriage or a friendship breaks up, and the people stop speaking to each other and act as if the other person no longer exists, that's "deading."

"Stupid" is different from "ignorant," which means not knowing. For example, regarding neurophysiology, all of us are more or less ignorant, but we're not stupid. If a scientist doesn't know a process or an equation, he may be ignorant. If he forgets where he parked his car, or runs out of gas, he is called, or calls himself, stupid.

A stupid person has no needs, other than to be ridiculed and punished until he or she gets smart, or good. But ridicule makes it difficult, if not impossible to think about the problem for which he or she was originally characterized as stupid. People then focus on the implications of stupidity, rather than the solution of the problem, and the "stupidity," the inability to function effectively, increases.

Children often call me stupid when I don't answer their questions—any questions. If I don't know how glass is made, and I say I'll find out and tell them, they tell me I'm stupid as soon as I say I don't know. I'm an adult and a teacher, and I'm supposed to know everything. But they also call their classmates stupid if they don't know the answer to a question like, "What happened on 'Sesame Street' yesterday?"

I often tell children that I made a mistake, and that mistakes are part of learning. I tell them that they should expect people to make mistakes, and that's why they put erasers on pencils. It's sad and destructive to teach children systematically to think of errors and mistakes as things they must guard and defend themselves against, rather than as an implicit stage in the process of learning how to do anything correctly. In effect, you don't learn how to do it correctly, until you do it incorrectly. A great teacher of drawing once said, "The sooner you make your first five thousand mistakes, the sooner you will be able to correct them."

It's very difficult to convince young children that it's O.K. to make mistakes, that mistakes can help them to learn. They don't believe me, because their experiences have taught them that it's not at all O.K. to make mistakes, and if they do, they'll be punished or ridiculed. They've learned to be frightened to make mistakes; that there is only one correct way to do everything. The most fearful children are would-be perfectionists who won't attempt any task unless they can do it perfectly, the first time, without an error. They are afraid to risk being "wrong"; being called "stupid"; and so their learning process is crippled, because to learn is to take chances.

MR. STERN: I think we, as parents, have to let children know we make mistakes, and that we're not perfect.

MRS. FINEHOLTZ: My children already figured that out. [laughter]

MR. FINEHOLTZ: A few weeks ago, I told my son that I made mistakes. He came back three or four times that week for reassurance that everybody makes mistakes.

ME: It's important to emphasize that mistakes are not only something human beings do because we're fallible, but because mistakes help us to learn. Help them to think about mistakes, theirs and others', that way, and you'll relieve them of the fear of being judged, and the guilt involved in judging. They'll begin to think, "O.K., I made an error. It didn't happen the way I wanted it to. I'll try not to make that mistake again, even though I'll make other ones. If I do make that mistake again, I'll recognize it as a problem to solve, not proof that I'm stupid, or bad, or that I have a need to make errors and be destructive." We can help children to think of themselves as learning by their errors, rather than thinking of themselves as incompetents who are stupid because they screwed up.

MRS. GARDNER: You hear all these theories, and you read the books, and that's fine when you're not really angry, or upset. When you're calm, you can use all those wonderful theories, but when you're mad, they go right out the window.

MR. FINEHOLTZ: Not necessarily. My son Chris is four, but we've established the principle of talking about differences. Sometimes, when I've had it, I'll say, "That's it! Go to your room!" He'll say, "You're not talking about it. We're supposed to talk about it." So I'll sit down with him, and we'll talk about it. We use this technique with each other.

MRS. GARDNER: But does it change anything?

MR. FINEHOLTZ: Absolutely. It changed both of us, and we use it back and forth.

ME: I've found that kids like to be taken seriously.

MANY VOICES: Yes. That's true. Me, too.

MR. FINEHOLTZ: They love the idea of going in and talking about problems. Sometimes, they tune you right out when you start to talk, but at least it establishes a way of working together, instead of against each other.

MRS. STERN: More often, we tune *them* out.

MRS. WEINER: You can also offer them a choice, if they're doing something noisy or destructive. You can say, "use the toy on the rug, or in the bedroom," instead of saying, "if you do that one more time, I'll have to take it away from you."

MRS. GARDNER: Sometimes, the child may be asking, though, "Are you going to let me get away with this? What are the limits to what you'll stand for before you start hitting or yelling?"

ME: Then you could help the child put the question in words by saying, "Are you asking me if I'll punish you if you don't do what I ask you to? I won't, but you can ask me that instead of acting out your question. Try to put your question in words." An acted-out question is a much more trying test than a verbalized one. It's easier for me to say, "No, I won't punish you," to a child who asks me if I'll punish him if he hurts me, but it's hard not to lash out at a child who comes up behind me and hits me with all of his might. The shock alone might cause one to act automatically, but it's those responses we'll have to change if we want our children not to make many of the mistakes we made.

Most of the time, children aren't conscious of the questions they're acting out. Sometimes, they'll laugh with relief if you can perceive their acted-out questions. Our techniques for relating to children derive from our attitudes and thinking; our conscious or unconscious ideas about ourselves and them. We make mistakes, we blow up, we keep trying. It's a long process, but it can be very pleasurable. If we relate to children rationally, they will relate rationally to us, and to all the people they encounter.

MRS. FINEHOLTZ: What do you do with a child who doesn't listen?

ME: Do you mean listen, or obey?

MRS. FINEHOLTZ: I don't understand.

ME: Parents often say to a child, "You're not listening to me!" when they mean, "You're not obeying me." The child probably *is* listening, or trying to, but he may not agree with what he hears, and may refuse to follow orders. That's commonly called "not listening."

MRS. WEINER: Are most of the children you're working with four and five?

ME: Yes.

MRS. WEINER: I'm wondering about something. All the examples you've given involve children who are obviously articulate, but the approach you're describing starts between parents and a child from the very beginning, from birth. What do you do with a two-year-old who can't tell you what he's asking, or feeling? The child can't understand what you're saying; they may understand a spanking much more than what you're saying.

ME: Well, it's true that a spanking gets an idea across to

them very directly. [laughter] But, actually, they *don't* understand it. I've seen children get hit for the first time. I know it's the first time because I know some parents who are committed to not spanking their children. Maybe they won't be able to keep this commitment as their children grow older, and test them more and more urgently to see if they'll punish, but until one child's—Sean's—third birthday, at least, they were able not to hit him, and to see that no one else did.

I saw him get hit for the first time, by another child, at a playground, and I'll never forget the look of shock and disbelief on his face. He couldn't believe this was happening to him. And even if a child isn't accustomed to getting hit, each time it happens he's still shocked that people do things like that. The only thing sadder than hitting a child who isn't used to getting hit, is hitting a child who is. It reinforces the idea that they can't count on people who love them not to punish them for acting out questions, and it raises the question, "If they punish me for something small, will they kill me for something big?"

Our society is built on a system of punishment and reward; small transgression, small punishment; large transgression, large punishment. Parents hope they can prevent large transgressions and large punishments meted out by society, by dealing out small punishments for small transgressions, early and often.

Lifetimes are spent, and lives wasted and lost, testing for the answer to the question; "Will you 'dead' me, or kill me, if I act bad enough?" We know we live in a world where people act irrationally and destructively toward each other; that's not news to anyone. What can we do to counteract this insanity?

We can try to help our children to think rationally, to act thoughtfully and compassionately, because wherever we look, they look, and see cruelty and destructiveness: on television, in the newspapers, on the streets, and even in the classroom, people threaten each other's lives, in jest, and in earnest.

MRS. JOHNSON: Do you find that television frightens children that much? I mean in terms of violence and hitting, and that kind of thing, even if they aren't being punished at home?

ME: Very much so. They constantly act out the violence of the TV programs in school. They learn from most programs they watch that people are violent, that they want to kill each other, and that they'll kill you if you turn your back on them for a moment. Even the cartoons.

MRS. JOHNSON: But that's true, isn't it, so how do you deal with the reality? We watched a program on Saturday that was recommended for children. A nice, white sea captain brings his boat to an island to trade, and hunt for sea otters. Within the first five minutes of the program, he kills the Indian chief on the island, and everyone else in sight. (The Indians are bad, not like us; they're like wild animals, so it's all right to kill them.)

You know, at this very minute, this is what's happening in Laos and Africa and the Middle East and South America, so what do you tell your children when they see the news on television? That it's not happening? It *is* happening! How do you help them with the fact that it is happening, it is crazy, and it *is* reality? When I was growing up, it was the other guys who were the destroyers; now it's us.

ME: How can we help the children to understand it, and change it, instead of just living with it? I tell children that I don't think people really want to hurt each other, but that they have been taught from the time they were little that they *do* want to hurt people.

We've just begun to learn that the function of the brain is to solve problems, and that this whole idea of good and bad is a mistaken theory that the brain developed in trying to learn what a human being is, what we need, and how we function.

Men have been cooperating for thousands of years to solve many problems, which shows that we can do it, but we haven't yet solved the problem of using death, or the threat of death, as a punishment to resolve differences. We aren't bad or stupid; we just haven't enough accurate information about our bodies and brains, how energy is organized in human form, but we will; you will.

MRS. GADDIS: Aren't those concepts too difficult for children to grasp?

ME: If they miss some of the particulars, they seem to get the general idea. Of course, when the children go home with their version of this information, their parents react—sometimes angrily, sometimes with hope and interest. Many parents are fascinated and excited with any new ideas which promise the hope of solutions to problems. I've found that if parents are willing to explore this new approach to old, familiar, and difficult problems, changes occur in the life of the child at school, and in the life of the family at home.

MRS. GARDNER: You're still talking about four- and five-year-olds. What about very young children? It seems to me that you're saying you can't start too soon.

ME: That's right, the earlier you start giving them accurate information about themselves and the world around them, the better they'll be able to cope with the maleducation they're sure to get when they go out in the world.

MRS. GARDNER: How soon is "earlier"?

ME: From the very first day they're born. Denah Harris once told me about a four-month-old baby who used to cry each time her mother left the room, but stopped when her mother came back in. Her mother constantly checked to see if the baby was hungry, if a diaper pin was sticking her, if she was wet, had defecated, or if she was lying in an uncomfortable position. The baby cried when she picked her up, and cried when she put her down. Her mother finally figured out that the baby cried when the mother went out of the room and turned the light off, but not when she went out and left the light on.

Mrs. Harris suggested she carry the baby over to the light switch, place her hand gently on the switch, and help her to move the switch up and down, turning the light on and off, while explaining that this is called light, which comes from electricity, which is energy, and that the thing they're moving together is called a switch, which makes the light go on and off. When the mother did this a few times, two things happened: participating in the experience comforted and soothed the baby, even though she didn't completely "understand" what was happening. Also, the experience and the procedure were recorded for future recall. There was no threat of punishment associated with it, it satisfied the baby's innate need to know, and the information was recorded by the cortex. If parents follow this procedure consistently, a baby will have a storehouse of nonmoral, nonpunitive information to call upon when she gets old enough to use language, and this will be the type and quality of information with which she'll start her conscious, conversational life.

Babies have a physiological need for the constant attention and investment of one or two people. It doesn't matter, of course, if those people are men or women, but those needs must be met. One of the primary needs, as important as food, is the need for information; sensory stimulation. The baby's brain needs accurate information constantly, as her stomach needs food. If she doesn't get it, she doesn't develop the way nature intended her to. Some people call it contact, some call it love; it's both of these and more. It's the constant investment in meeting the child's need for reassuring information. The need for accurate information, as a form of caring, may be greatest at birth, though it continues all through the life of a human being. Karl Pribram, the neurophysiologist, says: "Caring largely consists of being sensitive and responsive to changes occurring in the communicative context. Caring for someone is not so much doing something as doing it at the right time in the right place, when needs are felt and communicated."

MRS. GADDIS: God! I've already screwed up my kid then. I've made all the mistakes anyone here has mentioned, and some they left out! I've screamed at him, hit him, threatened him, and shut him up in his room. I didn't see any of what he did as asking questions, but just being a brat. I get the feeling I've done such a lousy job that I've ruined him for life.

ME (*smiling*): I know how you feel, but it's far from true. Besides making mistakes, you've already given your children a tremendous amount of accurate information. Start to tell them now that they are problem-solvers, and tell them how their brains and bodies work. Start to interpret their previously problematic and unacceptable behavior as their questions about reality and the punishment for wanting to know about it, and you'll be giving them the benefit of a rational education that few of us have had.

You'll probably find out, while you're at it, that you're hearing them for the first time. You'll be giving them a great head start because few people think about children this way. Children are rational, and they need accurate information and open communication. Their behavior is not directed against you; it is evidence of their desperate desire for empathy and help.

4

Problem-Solving

Problem-solving is a physiological process which begins in the brain. Unfortunately, many four- and five-year-old children don't know they have a brain, that it controls behavior, or even where it's located.

Instead of learning that our brains control behavior, and that we *learn* to act in ways which society categorizes as bad and good, most children are raised according to an implicit theory which leads them to believe that they are *born* good and bad. Rarely do children or parents realize that this is a theory which needs to be critically evaluated; by the age of four, and even earlier, most children have internalized it.

Most of us have been taught that children are good when they conform without question to what they are told by parents, teachers, clergy, doctors, and the other authorities in their lives. They are bad when they don't conform, don't follow directions, and raise questions in taboo areas. It is important to keep in mind that there are basically two ways a child can raise these questions: he can articulate them, if he has enough language; and he can act them out, if he doesn't have enough language, or has been taught that it's taboo to verbalize questions in some areas.

Children are discouraged from asking the questions; which their parents and teachers were taught not to ask—about sex, for example, or excretion, or birth and death. If they ask anyway, they're hushed up or diverted. A minority group child is quickly taught that asking questions publicly about how he differs from the majority can be dangerous to him and his family. Jewish children in Hitler's Germany were taught not to ask questions outside of the family circle. So were black children—at least until quite recently. Prior to 1960, if a black in the South dared to sit in the front of the bus, he was asking by his action, "Why can't a black person sit anywhere a white can?" and "What will happen to me if I sit here?" His questions were answered quickly, with punishment by law, or without it.

I worked in the nursery school to explore Harris's theory that children were acting out questions when they did or said things generally regarded as bad or taboo. These questions, it seems to me, fall into three very broad categories:

1. Is this a bad thing to do, and if so, why?
2. Why are people punished for doing it, and will I be punished, too?
3. Will the final punishment be death?

The first question is rarely recognized as such and even more rarely answered. Answers, when they do occur, are likely to be, "Bad people do bad things," "Because *I* say so!", "Don't bother me with stupid questions," "It just *is* bad, that's all," "How the hell should I know? Ask your mother (father, teacher)," or "You'll find out when you're older." The second question, about punishment, is almost always answered with a resounding "Yes."

Here is an example of a question within a statement. If a child says, "I hate vegetables!" that's probably a statement. If the child says, "I hate vegetables!" and throws the vegetables on the floor, that's a question—perhaps several. The questions are, "Will you punish me for throwing this on the floor?" or "Am I bad for throwing this on the floor?" or "Why did my friend throw her vegetables on the floor when I was at her house (and why did her parents punish her? Is she bad for doing that?)."

Children learn about behavior by imitating it. They will imitate behavior they find puzzling or frightening, as well as behavior they've learned gets rewarded. They try on behavior to see what it feels like. Children often "understudy" (the term is Harris's) the parent whose behavior puzzles, frightens, or worries them, more than they do the parent they are less fearful of. They often grow up unconsciously understudying their parents' disfunctional, troubling behavior, attempting to understand it without knowing they are asking questions. It's not the sins of the fathers and mothers that are passed on to the children, but rather all our unsolved problems.

One day four-year-old Tony took my hand on the way to the playground. He was pale and hunched over. He said he was frightened because Ellen had pushed him down. "She doesn't use her brain," he explained.

"She's frightened, too," I said. "We can help her to think."

"She's just stupid," Tony insisted.

"Is that what people say to you when you act like Ellen just did?"

"Yes," Tony admitted.

"Do you think it's true when they said it about you?"

"I don't know," he said, holding my hand tighter as we neared the playground.

Tony was beginning to think that if someone hit him, it wasn't because he or she was bad, but because the person might be frightened. If this was true about other children and adults, it might be true about him, too. He was able to describe Ellen's behavior in other than moral terms, but he was still ambivalent about whether she was bad for hurting him or whether she herself was frightened. By calling her stupid, he was still saying she was bad, but he was starting to explore the idea that people act as a result of what happens in their brains. The point is so important that it's worth repeating: all learned behavior—all behavior—originates in the brain.

Later, in the playground, Tony chased Ellen with a stick which he held like a bayonet. Ellen ran to me, screaming that Tony was going to stab her. I asked Tony where he saw people chase each other as he was chasing Ellen.

TONY: On TV.

ME: Would you like to know why people do that?

TONY: No!

ME: O.K.

[For many children, the only serious conversations they have had with adults are lectures, where rhetorical questions were posed by their teachers or parents. They are supposed to listen respectively and attentively, to benefit from the instruction, and not to ask any questions. When children said "no" to my offers of explanation, I stopped, and told them we could talk another time.]

TONY (*looking at me, indecisively, the stick in his hand*): I'm not a dum-dum.

ME: Nobody said you were.

TONY: Yes, they did. A lot of people said I was.

ME: Well, I don't think you are or anyone else is.

TONY (*handing me the stick*): Break it for me.

ME (*handing it back to him*): You do it.

TONY (*looking relieved*): O.K. [He broke it over his knee.]

Ken joined the class a month after school began. He was quiet and withdrawn for a few weeks, but then he began to terrorize the class. He hit and cursed the other children, tore their work, and threatened them. He was four but looked six. The muscles of his back and chest were already well developed, and as hard as steel wire. His coordination was extraordinary. He threw building blocks as accurately as a pitcher nicked the corner of home plate. He could consistently hit another child with a thrown block from thirty feet; sometimes he drew blood. He'd make sure I was looking, and then begin to hit another child. I moved quickly to intervene, attempting along with the other teachers, both to comfort the other child and stop Ken from hitting at the same time.

It took almost the entire school year to help Ken to begin to ask his questions in words instead of acting them out. He often lashed out without warning or apparent provocation, but when Ken wasn't tense and frightened, he was warm, friendly, and helpful to the teachers and children.

Alan, the only child to join the class after Ken, was quiet and gentle. He and his family had recently returned from living in France for two years, so Alan was trying to deal with culture shock, as well as being the new boy. Ken stopped hitting Eddie, and began to hit Alan, who had no idea how to respond. He couldn't mobilize for fight or flight. He froze under Ken's attacks, and wept, while Ken danced around him, singing "Baby, cry baby, stick your head in gravy!" I tried to introduce a third option to Alan: *thinking* as a way to solve problems. He had a big problem with Ken, even though he'd done nothing to bring it on. The child who's been hit must stop thinking of himself as a victim, because he can't solve problems from that position. Victims focus on their condition, instead of on solutions.

I told Alan that Ken hit him because Ken had been hit a lot, and was trying to understand *why*. Ken's parents told me that they hit him "all the time," because they thought that was the most effective way to retrain a "willful" child. Ken said he didn't understand why they always told him he was bad, and why they beat him. Sometimes they hugged and kissed him right after they punished him, and then, impulsively, hit him again. He found this terribly confusing and frightening, and imitated their behavior with his classmates. By repeating their punishment, he hoped to learn why his parents acted so strangely toward him. *Was he really bad?*

On Alan's first day in class, Ken hit him.

ME: "Why?"

KEN: I don't like him.

ME: But you don't know him. He's only been in the room for half an hour, and he hasn't even spoken to anyone.

KEN: I don't care. He's a dumdum and a fuckhead!

ME: Is that a way of saying someone's bad?

KEN: Yes, he's bad. I hate him!

ME: Are you afraid of him because he's new?

KEN: Yes, I'm afraid of him. I hate him.

Alan saw Ken hit other children, particularly children from other classes. We encouraged the children to visit each other's rooms, but Ken never visited. He leaped on children who did, cursing and screaming at them to get out. Eventually, we anticipated Ken's hitting, and were able to divert him until he got used to unfamiliar children, but by then, some of the other boys had begun to understudy Ken's behavior.

I told Alan that Ken was afraid of him and other children because they were unfamiliar. He seemed to be afraid of strangers in general. I asked Alan to watch Ken when anyone moved suddenly around him. He flinched, put his hands over his face to protect himself (you see this reflex in children who've been hit often, particularly without warning), and then lashed out. He was constantly on the defensive, constantly expecting to be hit, constantly fearful.

"It's hard to believe," I said to Alan, "but Ken is afraid you might hurt him. If he hits you, or looks like he's going to, tell him that you don't want to fight, that you don't want him to hurt you, and you don't want to hurt him. That's what he's afraid of. Tell him that you don't think he *wants* to hurt you."

ALAN: But, I *do* think he wants to hurt me!

ME: I know you do. We've all been taught that other people want to hurt us, and we want to hurt them, but it really isn't so. Of course, you don't have to believe that, and I don't want you to say anything you don't believe, but you do *hope* he doesn't want to hurt you, right?

ALAN: Yes, I hope he doesn't.

ME: Well, you can tell him that. If Ken says "Fuck you!," or "doodoo" [words Ken often said when he was fighting], it's his way of saying you're bad, and of asking why people say other people are bad. Tell him you're not bad, and neither is anyone else. Tell him we're all problem-solvers. I tell him that all the time, and if he hears it from you, it will help him to think about the ideas. He knows we all have brains which help us to solve problems. Keep telling him you don't think he's bad, because that's what he's most worried about. . . ."

ALAN: But, I *do* think he's bad.

ME: Alan, you learned that idea about him, like he learned it about himself, and about other people. I don't think it's a true idea, and what I'm telling you now are ideas that I think will change the way Ken acts toward you. You can think about them, and decide whether or not you want to say these things to Ken.

It's hard to talk to someone this way, [lifting Alan on to my lap] but it's even harder to be afraid that someone will hit you at any time, and not know what to do to stop them. Maybe you could just try this. I can't promise you it will work the first time, but it will work if you keep trying. There's no way I can tell every time Ken is going to hit you, and stop him from doing it. You and Ken will have to solve problems yourself when I'm not around. I stop him when I can, and I'm trying to teach him not to hit, but you can help. Tell Ken you don't think it's fun to fight, but it *is* fun to be friends and problem-solvers.

ALAN: But what if he says it's more fun to fight?

ME: You could tell him he learned that from people who only knew how to fight, but that fighting never solves problems.

ALAN: It's too much to remember.

ME: You don't need to remember it all. I'm telling you as much as I can, because this is a hard, painful problem for both you and Ken. Fighting isn't fun. It hurts when you lose, and even when you win, you get afraid that you might lose the next time. Then you'll be hurt like the person you just beat. You know, Alan, sometimes I think that Ken hits you so much because he sees how frightened you are, and it scares him that you're afraid of him.

ALAN: That's not a very good reason to hit somebody.

ME: You're right, it isn't. I don't think there's any good reason to hit anybody, but we have to convince Ken.

A nonproblem-solving response would have been to run, to fight, or to freeze, but the next time Ken attacked, Alan tried this kind of problem-solving. It was painful to watch Alan attempt to use these ideas, and then to see Ken batter him. I had to intervene again.

ME: Alan wants to be friends, Ken. He doesn't want to fight, or to hurt you.

KEN (*turning away, frightened, and then back to me, shrieking suddenly*): You're going to punish me!

ME: No, I'm not. Not ever, but I am going to help you to learn not to hit. I know you must feel frightened when you're hitting.

KEN (*screaming*): Yes, you'll punish me! Because I'm bad. You *should* punish me!

ME: Nobody in this school is going to punish you, Ken. [Ken began to cry, and as Alan and I watched in amazement, he began to punch himself, hard, in the head with his fists.]

KEN: If you won't punish me, I'll punish myself!

A moment before, I stopped Ken from punching Alan.

Now I stopped Ken from punching himself. A teacher, who was watching, said, "We all do that to ourselves, but he uses his fists."

Ken continually acted out questions about who was bad and who was good, and who should and shouldn't be punished. He wasn't the only nursery school child I saw hit himself in an anguish of pain and confusion. Ken punished himself often during the school year, but with decreasing frequency. Though this wasn't the last time he hit Alan, he never again attacked him with the same ferocity. From that day on, Alan stopped being Ken's special whipping boy.

A few days later, Ken asked to comb my hair, something he liked to do. He stood on a chair, and talked to me as he combed. "I don't want to hurt you," he said. "Tell me if it hurts. Nobody is supposed to be hurt." He held a small hand mirror for me to see the back of my head. "Anyway," he said, "me and Alan is getting to be friends."

"I'm glad," I said. "It's nice to be friends. It feels good to know that someone will help you when you need help."

"Yes," Ken said, "I think so."

I told him that the teeth of the comb were beginning to hurt my head. "I don't want to hurt you," he said, again. "If the teeth hurt you, I'll try to comb it with the lips."

Although I spent most days with Ken and his classmates, I occasionally visited other nursery schools. Because a friend of mine taught children of the same age as those I was working with, one day I visited her and shared yard duty. It was there, after a quiet morning, that I observed an incident that all parents of daughters dread.

Sarah and Ann, both five-year-olds, suddenly ran up to me, out of breath and wide-eyed.

"Teacher! Teacher! You know what just happened? Some big boys made us kiss their penises!"

They tugged me down to the other end of a block-long playground. They had been playing in a corner obscured by trees and a high cyclone fence. As we approached the area, three boys about twelve years old, wearing blue school blazers and gray pants, suddenly ran to the fence, threw their briefcases over, and began climbing frantically. Two other boys in blazers waited calmly for the girls and me to get nearer.

"Hey, kids," I yelled to the boys scrambling over the fence, "wait a minute. I'm not going to yell at you, I promise. I just want to talk to you for a minute."

One boy hooked his pants on the sharp points at the top of the fence and wriggled like a fish. I came nearer. He froze, then tore free, leaving a piece of his pants on the spike as he fell to the ground. He scrambled up and ran like the others, his coat straight out behind him like a flag.

"Hey, don't run," one of the boys who stayed behind yelled at his retreating back. "The man said he just wants to talk to you."

"What happened?" I asked.

They looked at the ground.

"You don't have to say. The girls told me some boys made them kiss their penises."

"It wasn't us," the larger boy said, biting his lip.

"If it was your friends, I'd like you to tell them something for me. Tell them I know they must have a lot of questions about sex, and that I could answer some of the questions for them. Tell them I'm not mad at them, and I won't tell on them, but if they keep asking questions about sex this way . . . if they did it—"

"The ones that ran; they were the ones who did it!" Ann yelled.

"Tell your friends that if they keep asking questions that way, most people who see them do it will probably punish them instead of answering their questions. I think they want to know what the penis is used for. They probably heard that people kiss each other's penises, and want to know why."

Ann and Sarah listened carefully.

"You really wouldn't get them in trouble?" the other boy said, looking up for the first time.

"No, I wouldn't. I think they need help with their questions about sex, but I also think it's harmful to these girls for your friends to ask their questions that way. The girls also have questions, about how bodies work, and what the different parts are used for, like the penis and vagina and clitoris. What the boys just did is very confusing and frightening to them."

Above the sound of the traffic, the girls' teacher was calling them to line up. "We have to go now," I said to the boys. "Tell your friends we can talk to each other about this."

Later, in the classroom, I explained to Ann and Sarah that the boys were asking questions about what penises and mouths are for, but that the boys needed to ask with words, instead of acting out their questions.

Months later, on another visit to the school in New Jersey, I again saw the three boys who ran. I noticed them first from a distance as they swung high in the air on metal swings, their jackets flying in the wind. I deliberately came nearer and stood where they could see me, but they didn't recognize me, or pretended not to. Finally I decided not to remind them about the incident with the girls; it was too long ago.

Another day I was called on for help at the playground used by my regular nursery school; it was quite a different situation and I was forced to intervene. Suddenly I heard some children yelling for help. "Those big boys are hitting us," they said. "They won't let us use the jungle gym. They hit Sam with a belt. Come and tell them to leave us alone."

Big boys, to four- and five-year-olds, usually means someone nine years old, but they pointed across the playground to a group of older boys I hadn't seen before. From a distance they looked about fifteen. The teacher who was with me didn't know who the boys were, but they looked rough, and she said there was no point in trying to say anything to them about hitting Sam; she was not going to get involved.

The other children urged me to talk to the boys. Sam sat crying on his teacher's lap, bare legs welted where the belt had hit him. I felt I had to make an effort. As I approached, I saw that they wore black leather and cutaway dungaree jackets emblazoned with gang colors. They were strangers to the neighborhood, fierce and sleek and more ominous than the local boys. Their jackets, decorated with bleeding hearts, flowers, daggers, and metal studs, said *Savage Lords.* I'd once seen a spray-painted subway message: Savage Lords—DTK. A friend explained that DTK meant Down (ready) To Kill.

I was too close to them to turn back. Four Savage Lords were spread out against the fence around the swings, their eyes slitted and dangerously blank. Children with the faces of mercenaries, their presence had emptied out the playground.

My four-year-olds peeked from behind me. "Tell them to leave us alone," one said. "Tell them you'll beat them up if they don't be good," another child said, making my blood run cold. I smiled weakly, as if to apologize for the child's remark.

"Is there some problem with the children?" I managed to get out.

"Yeah," the boy closest to me sneered. "Who are you?"

"I'm one of their teachers. Can you tell me the problem?"

"They were cursing at us and throwing sand, the little bastards," he said.

"One of them threw sand in my friend's face."

We were only a few feet apart, the little children around and between us. The Savage Lords were tense.

"Listen," I said softly, "I know you wouldn't want to

hurt children. You must have little brothers and sisters at home. These kids are only four and five. You know that little children hit and throw things because they see bigger people do it. They're trying to learn by copying. They don't want to hurt you, and I know you don't want to hurt them."

I held my breath. Two of the Savage Lords looked away, embarrassed.

"Well," one finally said, "they shouldn't mess with people. They could get hurt, and so could you."

"I know that, but part of a teacher's job is to take care of these children, to see that they don't get hurt, just like someone has that job with your brothers and sisters. If the children are causing problems for you, tell me, or one of the other teachers. We'll handle it."

We looked at each other and waited. "Don't talk in my face, mister," one of the boys said. "You're too close."

I backed away. "Talk to us if there's a problem," I said. "You don't want to hurt them."

All four of the Savage Lords looked either down or away. My heart beat fast, as one of the boys suddenly grabbed for the small Instamatic camera I was carrying.

"What's that for?" he asked.

"I'm taking some pictures of the children."

He let go of the camera. "Take our picture," he demanded. Then he smiled for the first time. "We're the Savage Lords . . . Can you get us in the newspaper?"

"No," I said, "I'm a teacher. I can't get you in the newspapers."

"It doesn't matter," he said. In the next instant four of the Savage Lords, looking for the first time like junior high school kids, threw their arms around each other's shoulders and squinted into the camera and the sun.

Maybe I wouldn't have confronted the Savage Lords if I'd had time to think about it, but the children, and their teachers, were watching me. We'd talked about problem-solving for eight months, and so they watched to see how I solved problems outside of the classroom. I had to try. The Lords let the children use the swings, and after twenty minutes, I stopped shaking.

I had approached these young street warriors without blaming them, without trying to make them feel bad or guilty, but most important, with the expectation, which I repeated to them, that they didn't *want* to hurt the children. They had hurt one child, and they might have hurt more, but they didn't. People are consistently relieved when you relate to them as if they don't *want* to act destructively, even when they *are* acting destructively. If I didn't proceed on that basis, my encounter with the Savage Lords most likely would have ended very differently. My fears, as well as the children's and teacher's, that people want to hurt each other, would have been strongly reinforced.

Sometimes a problem-solving transaction goes perfectly. For example, once I asked Ken why he'd hit Alan.

KEN: Because he won't be my friend . . .

ME: Did you ask him to?

KEN: No . . .

ME: Try asking him.

KEN (*turning to Alan*): Will you be my friend?

ALAN: Sure, I'll be your friend.

Ken and Alan went off to play together on the jungle gym.

As the children became more familiar with this approach, their solutions derived from a mixture of moral theory and new problem-solving circuits in their brains. One time, Ken knocked Annie out of the way in his rush to get some orange juice (moral theory, survival-of-the-fittest, me-first-never-mind-about-you), then turned quickly and caught her before she fell (cooperation, concern for the effect of one's actions on others). His teacher Glenda, who was watching, was delighted. "Ken," she said happily, "you're learning to be a problem-solver!"

At a meeting between some parents and me, four-year-old Evelyn's father told me that the week before, she had shocked him. The family was late and rushing to get out of the house. They had twenty minutes to catch the plane that would take them on vacation, but Evelyn was daydreaming, and moving very slowly. "I kept telling her to hurry up, but she just acted as if I wasn't there," her father said. "I was so frantic, I raised my hand to hit her. Suddenly, she looked up and pointed her finger at me. 'Careful, now,' she said, 'problem-solvers don't hit. They use their brains, and hitting isn't using your brain!'

"I thought I was hearing things," her father said. "I dropped my hand, and asked her where she heard all that.

" 'Steve told us,' she said."

Her father told her he didn't believe it. "What would you do," he asked her as he hurriedly jammed her left foot in her right shoe, "if your little sister took one of your favorite dolls away from you? How would you problem-solve that one?" Evelyn thought a moment. "I would walk over to her," she said, "talk to her like a problem-solver, and then I would kick her in the leg, grab the doll, and run away!"

Sometimes the attempt to solve problems raises additional problems for children. One child named Mitch told some boys who tried to fight with him that he didn't want to fight, and that they were problem-solvers, and so was he. They made a ring around him, taunted him, and told him he was bad. He insisted that he was a problem-solver, that he was neither good nor bad, and that they weren't either.

"Yes, you are!" they yelled, "you are, you are, you are!"

Mitch came home crying. "I'm *not* a problem-solver," he told his parents, who were trying to cooperate with my approach, "I'm bad, I'm bad!"

Mitch's experience presents a painful dilemma for parents and children. A child who tells another child that neither of them is bad is breaking a taboo, defying the tradition of looking at people with problems as bad and good. Mitch's classmates only knew the moral response, and they only had that to fall back on. Mitch defied a taboo by interpreting his classmates' behavior nonmorally. He also offered information that was so unfamiliar that other children might have thought him crazy (which is another way of saying "bad").

If Mitch conforms to moral theory, he'll act out rituals of bad and good for the rest of his life, as most of us do. If he continues not to conform to the moral theory, not to relate to himself or others as bad or good, he is likely to have the moral theory employed against him. There is no guarantee of safety in either position, but as a problem-solver, he can focus on living, instead of on avoiding death as a punishment. Either way, there are risks in this painful dilemma; he'll either run the risk as a problem-solver, or sit the risk, by living within the moral theory. Neither way is easy, but living as a problem-solver offers the hope of solutions.

One time, Ken saw Diane throw a pencil at me. Before I could say anything, he said, "If you want to ask Steve a question, do it in words, not by hitting. Try to problem-solve!" I was delighted. "Thanks, Ken," I said, "that was very helpful."

"Oh," Ken said, looking embarrassed, "that's O.K., baby!"

I told the children that problem-solving is learning, so in a way, making mistakes is a step in problem-solving. Even when people fight, they are *trying* to solve a problem, in the only way they know how—though it doesn't work. I didn't want children to think that problem-solving was just about fighting. Building, cooking, drawing, thinking, sharing, and helping their friends, parents, and teachers in ways that were beneficial to everyone and destructive to no one, were all ways of problem-solving.

There are more damaging punishments than hitting children, such as repeatedly telling them they are a burden or a curse, but I did find that children who were hit often, tended to hit often, striking back almost reflexively when another child hit them. The surest way to train a child to hit other children is to hit him. Children who aren't used to being struck, but haven't been taught any response, tend to freeze when they're hit, as Alan did. I tried to give such children another choice besides running away, hitting back, or standing still, frozen. The option was to see the fight as a problem to be solved, by empathy and by thinking.

One day Annie and Sarah began to test me, screaming hysterically, "Fuck, shit, doodie ass! Problem-solving is stupid, and so are you!"

ME: If you put your questions in words, I could answer them. This way I can't. [Annie began to hit me.] Are you worried that I'll punish you? [Annie had told me that her father slapped her face hard if she raised her voice or said four-letter words.] Did your father hit you lately?

ANNIE: Yes, last night, and you'll do it too, if we scream at you long enough.

To me, Annie's statement was clearly a question: "Will you punish me, too, if I test you like I test my father?" I told her that I thought that this was her question. She laughed instantly, warmly, for the first time that day, and hugged me, as she hit me lightly on the arm.

One day, Evelyn called me dumdum.

"Where did you hear that?" I asked.

EVELYN: On "Sesame Street." Isn't that where you get information on things, dumdum?

ME: I think you have a question about what dumdum means, and why people say that to each other.

EVELYN: No. My question is why I feel sad today. I need you to help me with my sister. She bites me; that is the problem. She bites me all the time, and I'm afraid. I told her what you said, that I wasn't food, that teeth were to chew food with, not to bite people, and she stopped for a while, but now she started again.

ME: Do you have a dog? [Most children who bit had dogs at home, and were understudying what the dogs did, trying to understand why. Children without dogs didn't bite nearly as often.]

EVELYN: Sure, dumdum, Her name is Daisy. She chews up everyone's shoes and bites people's toes. Not hard, though.

ME: Maybe your little sister learned to bite from Daisy.

EVELYN: Maybe. [pause] Would you write a letter home and ask my mommy not to spank me? I told her you were the Help Department.

Toward the middle of the year, Tony began to put his questions into words. "Why do people say bad words?" he asked one day, after months of constantly, obsessively repeating almost every four-letter word the two of us had ever heard.

ME: Because, when they were little, they needed to say words that talked about going to the toilet, how their bowels and bladders worked, or how babies were made, and people said they were bad. Their parents, all the grownups around them, didn't know they needed information.

TONY: I said *vagina* at home, and my mother slapped me. You told me it isn't a bad word.

ME: I told you *I* didn't think it was a bad word, but lots of people do. I'm sorry you got hit. You know, many people get upset when they hear children say words about taboo things. A taboo is something that people say isn't nice to talk about, or do. Probably, your mother thinks if she punishes you for saying *vagina*, then you won't say it in front of other adults, and get punished more. She's trying to protect you. It's very confusing, isn't it?

TONY: But, you said it was O.K. to say those words . . .

ME: No, I didn't. I said there were scientific words for the things we did with our bodies. They're not bad or good words, and neither are the words that people use in the street. I don't think there are bad or good words, or that taboo words like *shit,* are bad or good either, but most people do. I don't think it's O.K. to say any taboo words around people who get upset hearing them. It's O.K. to ask me about them, because I think you need that information. Different people think different ways about many things. You'll learn who you can say which words to, or in front of. That's confusing, but it's real. We need to learn how to approach people with our questions so they don't get frightened or upset.

Terry and Ken fought to spend time with me. Ken never knew his father, Terry saw his father only occasionally. Ken usually won their continuous fight. Terry was calmer during the week that Ken was out of school with a virus, and played quietly with the other children. The day Ken came back, Terry screamed all afternoon. He threatened to throw the cardboard knife he'd made that day at me. I told Terry I thought he was frightened because Ken had returned and that I'd finally heard the question he was acting out.

"Are you afraid that Ken is going to hit you?" I asked Terry.

"No," he replied, "I'm afraid because people do such bad things to each other."

He wouldn't admit he was afraid of Ken, but he stopped screaming almost immediately. He hugged me, and climbed on my lap. He told me I was his friend. Often, the children hugged and kissed me immediately after I acknowledged or helped them to deal with a fear they were experiencing.

It took me some time to learn not to ask a child, "What's the matter?" When I did, or varied it with "What's wrong?" children withdrew. They reacted as if I'd said, "What's wrong with *you?* What's the matter with *you?*" We can understand this if we try to imagine our own reaction when we are sad or upset and someone asks, "What's the matter?" A better question and a better way of learning about the problem is, "Why are you crying?" or "What happened?" or "Would you tell me what you're thinking now? You seem sad or worried." Such questions elicit answers. Children like to hear specific and personal questions which don't imply that the problem is anyone's fault, particularly when there has been an argument between them. Children learn that if something painful or unfortunate happens, it must be *somebody's* fault.

Another time Ken suddenly began boxing with Annie, who couldn't defend herself because she was much smaller. Before we could stop him, he gave her a bloody nose. Annie began to cry, and Marilyn picked her up to comfort her.

Tony, who had seen the fight, immediately tried to make sense of the situation. "You know," he said, "people who box aren't using their brains. Neither are the people who write about it in the newspaper."

I asked him to talk louder because the room was so noisy.

"Yeah, it is noisy," he agreed. "I wish I'd brought my earmuffs."

Ken began to yell.

KEN: You think I'm bad, badder than a monster. You'll hit me on the head.

ME: You know we won't hit you, Ken.

KEN: The other teachers will hit me.

ME: They won't.

KEN (*shouting*): I love to break things! [His questions were all about being taught he was bad.]

ME: I think you were taught that you love to break things. I don't think you do. You're really asking me if we'll punish you for hitting Annie, and if you're bad, and if you like to break things. I've seen you make things, too.

KEN: You tell my mommy that. She asks me sometimes when I'm bad if I'm trying to kill her!

One afternoon, some children noticed a jagged scratch on my finger. I'd taken my cat, Christmas, to the veterinarian, and she bit me when I tried to hold her down so the vet could give her some medicine. She's a very gentle cat and had never bitten me before. I explained to the children that even the gentlest animals can hurt someone when they panic, and that when people lash out and hurt someone, they are in a panic, too.

Five-year-old Vinnie, quick and violent one moment, affectionate and gentle the next, told me he was going to start karate classes. He said it was his parents' idea. His father was a clinical psychologist who told me that Vinnie had instructions to "punch anyone that gave him a hard time." Vinnie interpreted this to mean any child who differed with him.

ME: Do you want to take karate lessons?

VINNIE: Of course I do. That way I can beat up more kids, faster, stupid!

ME: Wouldn't you rather learn to use your brain to solve problems? Your brain controls the muscles you use for karate.

VINNIE: No more of your old stupid problem-solving . . . [pause] Why *do* people hit each other, anyway, and say bad words? Are they all bad?

ME: No, but people haven't learned to use their brains to solve problems, yet, but they will. All of us will.

VINNIE: I'm learning how to use mine, but I'm going to learn karate, just in case!

Another time, Vinnie asked me what I would do if he

stuck me with a knife. Verbalizing this question was a big step for him, because he usually acted his questions out.

ME: The first thing I'd do is bleed, probably, then I might cry. I'm sure it would hurt.

VINNIE: I mean, would you punish me; would you kill me?

ME: No, of course not. You know, people who carry knives are afraid other people will hurt them. [Vinnie occasionally brought small penknives to school. We asked his parents to make sure that he stopped.] Are you afraid people will hurt you?

VINNIE: You're goddamned right I am.

Many people are concerned about the effect of overinterpreting reality for children; the danger of controlling, and robbing children of the opportunity to learn for themselves. What is too much interpretation, and what is too little, is an open question, but children interpret all of their experiences according to *some* learned frame of reference. We all do. Parents provide most of this frame of reference, consciously or not, more by what they do than by what they say. We learn from childhood that the "role" of parents is to teach their children what the culture says is "right from wrong."

Our silence in the face of violent or confusing events is, of course, not an explanation, but children see it as an interpretation. They assume that we neither notice the events, nor think them worthy of notice. They then learn to deny the effect of this violence and confusion upon them, as we did, and interpret our indifference as a sign of unconcern, or even tacit approval.

We and our children should decide mutually how much to interpret, and when and when not to. After their first few years, much of what they see and learn takes place away from us. We'll have an opportunity to help our children interpret what they see, hear, and think, if we encourage them to bring these experiences back to us for discussion, and if we listen without making moral interpretations. The surest way to cripple or impede a child's ability to interpret reality is to condition him to interpret it in ways that avoid our moral disapproval and assure our moral approbation.

If we can't talk to each other, and to our children, we can't solve problems. The idea that I explored with children, that people are neither good nor bad, that this is a theory and not an unquestionable truth, and that human beings can solve all their reality problems by using their brain cortices according to their innate functional potential, are contrary to the ideas the human race has lived by up to the present time. If adults punish children and hurt and kill each other not because they choose to, or need to, but because they were taught to, then they can learn not to. When we were children, no one understood how frightened we were, but we now have the chance to understand how frightened our children have learned to be.

Using this problem-solving approach with your child can sometimes be discouraging. One would need an entire community of support for it to be *maximally* effective. That means neighbors, teachers, friends, the children's playmates, their parents, our in-laws, and particularly our parents (their grandparents)—all dealing with each other in the same way.

It's discouraging to learn that grandma responded to your child's acted-out questions about four-letter words with a slap in the face, or a spanking—the same response she might have given you. There are always those well-meaning grocers who will say to your preschooler, "Put up your dukes and fight like a man," and friendly policemen who will laughingly offer to put your child in jail for you if she's bad. Among the children with whom I have worked there was a real obsession about jail. They threatened each other with it constantly, and solicited assurance from me that they wouldn't be going there if they were bad.

Not so long ago, it was a common practice to lock children up in school coat rooms, or in closets at home, to teach them a lesson. This, of course, is a form of jail, and also activates the child's fears, based on his misconceptions about death as a conscious experience—that is, being buried alive for being bad.

When I was about five, someone, I can't remember who, took me on a visit to our local small-town precinct house. There, after a brief tour, one of the officers locked me in a cell. I screamed for a few minutes and implored him to let me out; when he released me, I'm sure he thought it was a harmless joke.

There will be teachers who will tell your children they are bad, and other adults and children who will insinuate that they are, if they don't actually accuse them. But if you stick to this nonmoral approach to your children it will work, perhaps only in small ways at first. But you *will* be relieved of your fear that you and your children are good and bad, and must be punished and rewarded. So will your children.

If this approach doesn't work for you, the important thing is not to blame yourself. With all of your expectations and best efforts, remember that you are bucking an entire culture that believes and acts on the idea that all children, all human beings, are mixtures of good and evil. Nevertheless, I have found that even limited success with this approach gives families renewed hope and new confidence in their own potential to solve some of the many problems between parents and children. I have also found that if we help the children to think of themselves as problem-solvers, and to cooperate with each other and us, they will do the rest.

5

Physiology: The Signals of Fear

Children are fascinated with the way the human body works: theirs, yours, mine, and each other's. When I told the boys and girls at the nursery school that I'd try to answer any questions they had about how people and animals were put together, they besieged me with their questions, statements, misconceptions, and fears.

I started from scratch. In bookstores and libraries, I searched out any materials that might explain birth, death, or physiology to children. Some of the books were written for children; most were not. My wife had a copy of Walter B. Cannon's classic, *The Wisdom of the Body,* which tells "how the human body reacts to disturbance and danger and maintains the stability essential to life." Cannon's theme is that our bodies are tremendously strong and adaptable and can withstand great stress and shock. I wanted the children to learn this, to gain confidence in the resiliency of their bodies, their ability to "take it." They needed this confidence to overcome the fear I saw so often—a fear that they had learned—that a cut or scratch or sting would lead to serious illness or even death.

I bought a copy of Guyton's *Physiology*, the only physiology book I knew which focused on the optimum function of the body and not on its pathology.

When a child shows us some minor cut or bruise, we are likely to say—as was said to us years ago—"Oh, that's nothing." In this way we hope to reassure the child, and ourselves. We may be reassured, but the child isn't. He has neither the physiological information nor the years of getting scratched, burned, bruised, cut, and then healed that we've had. To us, it's "only" a scratch; to a child, unless he acquires some information about the toughness of his body to substitute for the life experience he can't possibly have yet, a scratch is a source of fear and worry, a potential threat to his life. Some of the children in my group said they thought that all their blood might come out of a tiny scratch on their hand. I taught the children that blood clots, a useful bit of information since they might otherwise believe that any blood that flows out of them will never stop. Most important, the information I gave them focused on how strong they were. The more they knew, the less they would panic when something happened to their bodies, and the quicker they would heal.

After studying anatomy and physiology on my own, I began working with two or three children at a time. We read books they chose from the pile I brought to school, and I answered their questions instead of teaching them a series of lessons. After a while, a child who had a stomach ache or a cut finger, or who was developing chicken pox, would ask me to get out one of "the body books," which is how they referred to our physiology library. The children took the books home and kept them, which they didn't do with story books. Even though I had to replace the books, I was happy to supply them with this information.

Later in the year, my wife, Barbara, and I brought transparent plastic scale models of the human body, called "The Visible Man" and "The Visible Woman," and managed to put them together.

The children were thrilled when I brought The Visible Woman to class. Nothing in school excited them like the chance to take her apart. She was better than a movie or a Halloween party. She even had a detachable uterus enclosing a tiny fetus. (These parts were packed separately in a plain brown box.)

By the end of his first day at school, The Visible Man was missing his pancreas, half of his heart, and one small plastic eye. The Visible Woman was delivered of her fetus, and it disappeared. I thought it had become the smallest addition to some child's doll collection, but the fetus showed up a few days later under the aquarium.

I tried to supervise the children as they became familiar with the models, but it proved impossible. Everyone wanted to touch them at once. I tried to make them take turns, and vainly yelled, "One at a time!" but The Visible Man and Woman were mobbed like political candidates. Fortunately, the parts were replaceable.

Later, a friend gave me an already assembled and painted model of a human skull, brain enclosed, which she named "Homer." The children quickly learned the location and simple function of the cerebrum, cerebellum, cortex, and medulla, but after a few weeks, Homer had a great fall from the top of a cabinet. I put him there, thinking no one would find him, but some children spotted him, and climbed up to do a "brain operation" on him. The ensuing accident made Homer's brain and skull inoperable.

I experienced a child's intense fascination with physiology during the summer weekend when Barbara and I assembled and painted The Visible Woman while staying with friends. Brian, their four-year-old son, watched us and listened carefully as I read the complicated assembling instructions to

Barbara. We took turns fitting the bones together and putting the organs in place. Brian, usually very active, listened quietly.

His mother, Ellen, was in the kitchen making dinner. "Don't you know four-year-olds can't understand a lot of words?" she yelled, over the sound of the running water. "You have to show them, not tell them. My God, that sounds like a textbook for doctors!"

Ellen couldn't hear our answer and we were almost finished, so we kept working, while Brian went on observing.

A few hours later, a friend of Ellen's arrived, along with her daughter, who was Brian's age.

"Do you know how your esophagus works?" Brian greeted them. He showed them the completed Visible Woman, and began to explain the parts and their functions, almost verbatim. He remembered most of it, and he understood the relationships. We were all amazed, but my experience in the school had convinced me that most children share Brian's ability to retain physiological information.

Sometimes I was able to be useful in quickly clearing up a misconception. For example, I had noticed that when Scott played with other children and got very excited, he would squeeze his thighs together, grit his teeth, and close his eyes, but he wouldn't stop what he was doing to go to the toilet.

ME: Scott, do you have to urinate? You look very uncomfortable?

SCOTT: A little . . .

ME: Why don't you go?

SCOTT: I don't want to let the cork out.

He told me later, after more squeezing, grimacing, and standing on his toes while he arched his back, that he really thought, "There's a cork inside my stomach that holds back the weewee."

I explained to him that there wasn't a cork, and that his urine wasn't in his stomach, but in his bladder. He asked me how it "worked." I took out a body book, and we explored the way his sphincter muscles and urogenital system function. He was soon relieved.

Another time, a group of children made a ring around Betsy, and teased her for wetting her pants. Her face turned red and she wept bitterly. She ran to me with her arms outstretched, begging to be picked up. She buried her face in my shoulder, sobbing.

"Betsy is a baby, Betsy is a baby!" the children chanted, as Betsy cried even harder.

"Betsy isn't a baby," I said, "and babies aren't the only ones who cry. She feels very sad right now because you don't understand what happened. You're calling her a baby because babies wet their pants a lot. The reason they do is that their muscles aren't strong enough to hold back their urine. A muscle that everyone has called a sphincter, holds back the urine, and your sphincters are stronger than a baby's. When you were babies, you hadn't learned yet how to use your sphincter muscles to hold back urine. You learned it was bad to wet your pants. Your parents got tired of changing your diapers over and over. They wanted you to hurry up and get big, so you'd stop making in your pants, and they could stop having to change you."

"But Betsy is four!" a child yelled.

"Sometimes even four-year-olds have an accident. They forget to go, or they hold their urine in too long, and their muscles can't hold it any more. Sometimes grown-ups wet their pants, too."

"Did you ever?" Eddie asked.

"Sure I did."

"Ohhh," Eddie said, "then you're a fuckin' baby!"

"Baby, baby, stick your head in gravy!" the children chanted.

"Eddie, wetting your pants doesn't make you a baby. A baby is someone who's only lived a very little while. Doing something that a baby does doesn't make you a baby. You can see I'm not a baby, and neither is Betsy. Are you saying that anyone who wets his pants is a baby because you think it's better to be a little boy than a baby?"

"Yeah," Eddie said, "damn right!"

"It isn't better," I said, lifting Betsy down, "just different. Of course, it's a pleasure to be able to do more and more things, and you can do a lot of things babies can't do yet. But they will, just like bigger kids can do a lot of things you can't do yet, but you will."

Eddie looked skeptical as the ring around Betsy and me broke up, but a few weeks later I heard him explain to some friends in another class how they could use their sphincter muscles to hold back their urine. He said that boys and girls could both do it. Although he remembered the word sphincter, he pronounced it 'shrinker,' but that was the only error he made.

Just as children have been treated cruelly out of ignorance, they, too, can be incredibly cruel to one another. If they've learned that their bodily functions are ridiculous and shameful, they will ask questions about why this is so by ridiculing other children. If all children learn to interpret these taunts as questions, they will be much less vulnerable to this ridicule. One thing is certain: they will all be ridiculed sooner or later, no matter how hard they might try to avoid it by conforming. The best protection against this kind of universal insensitivity is accurate information, so that the child who is the target does not feel a victim, and doesn't see his tormenters as victimizers, but rather as fellow sufferers of crippling ignorance, who are desperate for information they need but can't get anywhere.

Sometimes I became frantic, trying to answer so many questions coming all at once. One day, for example, Eddie asked me how his Adam's Apple worked. I didn't know. As I went to get the body book in order to find out, Bobby asked me if a man could be a cowboy and a daddy at the same time, while his twin sister asked me what her stomach did with food. Joan wanted to know how her heart worked, and all the while Eddie tugged on my arm, saying, "Let's get the body book." Then Paul came up to say that some of the children were playing dead, and would I show him pictures of the mummies in the *Time-Life* body book? "I know the page they're on, and everything!" he exclaimed. But by this time Lizzie had grabbed my other arm, and was asking me how people made babies. Suddenly, I felt overwhelmed. My voice began to sound shrill. Marilyn told me not to talk so loud. "Bend over," she said quietly, "or crouch down to talk to them. Remember, you're twice their size."

Ken resolved everything, in a way, by punching Paul. A shelf fell over on the other side of the room with a great crash. As Marilyn, and Glenda Burns, her assistant, rushed to see that no one was hurt, I tried to comfort Paul and restrain Ken at the same time. Ken needed comforting, too. I held him as gently as I could, realizing that I couldn't answer everyone's questions at once, and meet all their needs.

Sometimes they asked questions by showing me, or each other, their genitals—in spite of the taboo against this. Sometimes they asked to see mine, a request I politely and consistently turned down, although they thought my reasons weak.

"Ask your mom or dad," I would say. "Remember, all women's genitals look a lot like each other's, and all men's genitals look very much the same."

"I saw my mommy's and daddy's," some answered; others came back with, "Dad won't let me, so now I want to see yours."

They would run to me with their cuts, a look of terror on their faces because they had seen blood dripping. As I cleaned the cut, I explained again how strong their bodies were, and that the cut would heal more quickly if they tried not to panic, and would learn about the healing process with me. Panicking, I explained, would make their hearts beat faster, which would make their blood flow faster, but that some bleeding *was* necessary to clean the cut. I told them that their bodies contained a chemical called coagulin, which would automatically stop the bleeding faster if their brain was functioning in a nonpanicked way.

Children are often incredulous about things they've seen which we've come to take for granted. A three-and-a-half-year-old boy once asked me, "Why do women put paper between their legs to make themselves bleed?"

Sally told me that babies were born from their mother's behinds. "Where did you hear that?" I asked her.

"My friend told me," she explained. "Is it true?"

I told her it wasn't. She said she'd like to see where they *did* come from, in the body book.

Another time, Eddie wanted to know why ladies have breasts:

ME: So they can feed milk to their babies, if they have babies.

EDDIE: If men have penises, why don't ladies have them?

ME: Ladies have uteruses, vaginas, and urethras. If they have babies the baby will have a place in the mother to grow—that's the uterus; and the urethra is what the woman's urine passes through after it leaves the bladder.

EDDIE: Are you bullshitting me?

"Steve, how come you're always teaching us about our bodies?" Eddie picked up the conversation a few afternoons later.

ME: Because if you learn how your body works, you'll be less afraid that it will stop working if you're hurt or frightened, and more sure of how strong it really is.

EDDIE: But we'll still die some day though, right?

ME: Yes, but when you know enough about how to use

your brain so that it works normally, you'll be less afraid of dying.

"Nice," Eddie said, and proceeded to sing a song he made up, which I came to call "Eddie's Blues." Its only verse went, "When your brain dies, you die, oh yes, when your brain dies, you die; life is over when your brain dies, and that ain't so good."

Worse, though, is to be afraid that your brain lives on when you die.

The children continually required information about illness and their bodies. One day Scott seemed agitated and preoccupied, and I asked him what he was thinking about. "I'm going to have my tonsils out tomorrow," he explained, "and I'm worried."

We looked up tonsils in one of the body books, and learned where the tonsils were located and what the author thought their function was (there is some dispute about this). After we had gone through all the book had to say, Scott suddenly said, "I was only joking you about my tonsils. I had them out last year."

"Then why did you tell me you were going to have them out tomorrow?" I asked.

I felt foolish, and annoyed that a four-year-old had put me on. I tried never to tease the children unless they knew I was teasing, and I hoped they'd treat me the same way. The "put on" seemed to me a way of keeping distances between people. I didn't realize that it can sometimes be a way of asking questions. A minor penalty for taking children seriously is a partial loss of one's sense of humor. One becomes literal-minded, and drops one's guard against deliberate distortions of reality. One tends to believe everything one hears, and assume that if the communication isn't accurate, at least it's meant to be.

It turned out that Scott had questions about his experience: "When we went to the hospital last year, my mommy lied to me. She told me we were going to my grandma's, and all of a sudden, we were at the hospital. I got so scared, I forgot why I was there. I thought I would die there."

My momentary resentment vanished. I remembered how, when I was eight, my parents tried to get me into the hospital for a tonsillectomy, without telling me where I was going. We didn't have a car, and I knew something was wrong when a taxi pulled up in front of our house, and my mother said, "Let's go for a ride."

"Where?," I wanted to know.

"Well," my father stammered, "we're going to go to the hospital, and you're going to . . . going to have . . . your . . . your tonsils out!"

I let go of his hand, and took off down the block. There was an old, deserted golf course behind our house, and I made for that. Though I was only eight, and my brother was sixteen, I experienced such a rush of adrenalin that it took my brother ten minutes to catch me and drag me, screaming, to the taxi. I cried as if I were on my way to my execution.

In the hospital, all I remember is the impassive faces of the nuns, and the unforgettable, heavy smell of ether. As I lay in a cubicle, sobbing, a figure in black and white came to give me an injection.

"Lift up your nightgown!" the nun commanded. "You're going to get an injection."

In her hand she held what looked to be like the longest, thickest needle in the world.

"I want my mommy," I sobbed.

"I have no patience for you," she said through tight lips. "Your mommy's gone home."

Roughly yet efficiently, she whipped the nightgown up around my head and plunged the needle into my buttock.

Even the ice cream I got later on didn't make up for my shock at my parents' duplicity and the insensitivity of the Sister.

Neither Scott's mother, nor my parents, knew any other way to help a child through this terrifying experience, but at least I knew how Scott felt. Parents can intervene in the process, and diminish their child's sense of isolation by insisting that they be permitted to stay overnight in the hospital with him. They should also insist on being with the child when he receives injections or any medical attention which is likely to frighten him. Many hospitals have accommodations for parents to stay with their children; those hospitals that don't should hear about it from parents.

Parents can also ask that the doctor, nurse, and technician explain what they are doing to the child, and why. The question of the child's right to refuse any medical procedures which he finds frightening is too complex to go into here, but this question involves his rights as a human being, as a child, and as a patient.

It's difficult to insist on human treatment for our children—and ourselves—when we've been conditioned from childhood to follow doctor's orders and hospital regulations; it's difficult, but it would help children through a potentially frightening experience, and give them confidence in their parents' ability to solve problems and help them in a crisis situation.

On the playground one day, Dwayne complained of a cut. There was a tiny hole on his hand, his epidermis was slightly scraped, and there was a pinpoint of blood. I explained to him that he had two layers of skin—the corium, or dermis, underneath, and the epidermis, on top. Then there were little tubes called capillaries through which blood traveled, and his body had many of them. Once in a while, a few broke. "That's what happened this time," I said, "but your body will heal it up quickly." Dwayne seemed mostly reassured, as the children usually were by such an explanation; after hearing it once or twice, they stopped being afraid when they got a scratch and began explaining to the other children how skin healed.

But there were other times when I had no idea as to how to answer a child's question. There was the occasion, for example, when we passed a boy in the park and the children noticed his withered arms and legs.

ANNIE (*quietly*): What happened to that boy?

MARILYN: Something happened to his muscles.

ANNIE: Did he get shots? [Did she know about polio?]

MARILYN: Probably.

ANNIE: Does that happen to a lot of children?

ME: No, but it happens to some.

[Annie's real question probably was, "Will that, or could that, happen to me?" She might also have wanted to know if what happened to the boy was a punishment.]

ANNIE: Why does it happen to some children?

ME: I don't know, Annie.

When I didn't know the answers to the children's questions, I told them so.

One day Teddy complained that one of the children had hit him on his burn-scarred arm.

ME: I don't think he knew it was your arm that was burned.

TEDDY: I don't want him to come near me again.

ME: Why?

TEDDY: He'll kill me. He'll hit me with a car.

ME: Did you ever see anyone hit by a car?

TEDDY: Yes, near my house. A boy got hit by a car and got his teeth knocked out.

Teddy was asking if a child who would hit him in such a

sensitive area would do it on purpose, would hurt him to the point of killing him, and whether cars were an instrument of death, and if so, why.

When Dwayne fell down and scratched himself again on the playground, he asked me for a tissue. Suddenly his nose began to run, though he didn't cry. Denah Harris told me once that a runny nose could be unshed tears. I asked Dwayne if he were frightened. "Yes," he said. "I am. Aren't you?"

Besides runny noses, there were other physiological signs of fear I came to recognize. Eating to the point of gorging was one. Ken, particularly, over-ate when he was frightened or anxious. One day he began to scream and hit the other children. He spanked Annie. I held him, and talked quietly to him, but he cried and shook his head wildly from side to side, moaning, his eyes closed. Finally, he bit and kicked me, and I felt myself getting frightened and tense; squeezing him too hard, restraint verging into punishment. I tried to hold him more gently, to counter-act my tension.

I had learned from my family and my culture that when children acted like Ken (when I'd acted as he was acting now), they needed and deserved to be punished. I was frightened by his wild, destructive anarchy. I'd been punished when I acted like him; he should be, too, according to my experience—I had learned about how adults treat "bad" behavior. Now I had to fight consciously to evaluate these punitive techniques. I surely couldn't help Ken to solve any problems as long as I thought he was doing these things because of the evil in him. This would only be acting out what had been done to me and automatically reinforcing it. Ken screamed and cursed at me to let him go; the other children gathered around us, frightened and worried. I told Ken I'd let him go if he'd agree not to hit. He nodded, but when I let go, he raced over to Annie, hit her, and ripped up her drawings.

This was the last straw for Glenda, a teacher who was usually calm and relaxed. She shook Ken, pushed him against the wall, and yelled, "We don't do that in here, do you hear me?" Ken stopped, and looked subdued and frightened. When the children drifted back to their play, he went to the cookie jar, and stuffed his mouth with cookies, crying softly to himself.

I saw children eat like this many times, right after being frightened by something. This kind of eating seemed to be a sign of fear, in children and in myself. If I'm anxious, I eat a lot without feeling at all hungry; however, if I'm extremely anxious, I can hardly eat at all. This may be one reason children have eating problems, and yet some parents think they must force them to eat, which exacerbates the problem. If children aren't eating because they are worried about something, the parents' urging will only make them more uncomfortable.

After Terry spent one morning playing hospital and death games, I watched him drink seven glasses of juice. Usually, he only drank one. I began to watch for a cause-and-effect relationship between the content of the games the children played and the amount of liquid they drank. The frightening games, even when no running was involved, seemed to cause children to drink more juice and water. Their thirst also increased after listening to a scary story, or telling one.

It's possible that a child who is unwilling (really unable) to go to sleep at night may ask her parents for all those glasses of water because she is really afraid to go to sleep, and the homeostasis of her body is affected by her fear. The fear might cause her cells to dehydrate slightly, and her throat to become dry. This may explain why the timeless ritual of asking for a glass of water at bedtime may not be a total ruse.

Danny wanted to know how his stomach worked.

"I don't know why it is," he said, looking at the floor, "but every time I start to come to school, my stomach hurts."

ME: What are you thinking about before you come to school?

DANNY: I think about how Ken always hits everybody. [Ken heard his name. As if on cue, he rushed over and hit Danny.] Hey, don't hit me! I wasn't saying nothing bad about you. I just wish you would stop hitting, because it scares me.

KEN (*looking puzzled*): "You mean you're a scared sucker, right?"

DANNY: I'm a problem-solver. I'm trying to be friends.

Ken paused, not knowing what to say or do next. Danny wasn't playing the role of victim. After a moment, Ken walked away toward the cookie jar. Danny went on talking, but when Ken saw us watching him, he shoved another cookie in his mouth, and bawled out, "What are you looking at me for? I'm scared, but I ain't hitting!"

It was when Sally's parents' marriage was breaking up that she began to laugh all the time, a bit hysterically. One day, she came to school rigid with fear, her eyes staring open, the pupils shimmying from side to side. I used to think that descriptions of frightened eyes, sad eyes, and loving eyes were a writer's device, but I learned a lot from looking directly at the children's eyes. When they were relaxed, their eyes were bright and alert, the pupils fixed. When they were frightened, their eyes bulged, shifted, or looked glazed, or the pupils oscillated rapidly from side to side, like Sally's.

As she lay on the mat in the book corner, rigid as a soldier at attention, I stroked her hand and talked softly to her. Every few minutes, a convulsion shook her body. She was terrified beyond crying, frozen with fear.

Suddenly, she hit me and began to laugh.

ME: Why did you hit me?

SALLY: My daddy did that to my mommy last night. He's a bad daddy.

ME: Do you know what problem-solving is?

SALLY: Yes. To help someone.

ME: Let's solve this problem. Do you know anyone who laughs when they're frightened?

SALLY: My daddy laughed when he hit my mommy, but he wasn't frightened. My daddy's not scared of anything.

ME: I think maybe he was frightened . . .

SALLY: No. He's just bad, not frightened. Mommy said so. My little brother laughs when he hits me, too.

ME: Did you ever see your daddy hit your mommy before?

SALLY: Lots of times, but not so hard.

ME: Was your brother there, too?

SALLY: Yes.

ME: Maybe that's where he learned to laugh when he hits you, and why you laughed when you just hit me.

SALLY: Shut up!

ME: I know it's painful. Do you want me to stop talking about it? [By now, Sally had stopped shaking, and looked calmer.]

SALLY: No. Keep talking about it.

Shortly after this, I met Sally's mother briefly. I told her that her daughter was suffering intensely from the problems she was living through at home, and that maybe we could talk about ways to help Sally in school.

"I'm suffering with this thing, too," Mrs. Held said. "Sally will have to wait. I know that sounds cruel, but I work full time, and then come home to cook and clean and fight with her father. I have no time to help the kids: I can hardly help myself. Maybe after some of this is over, we can talk. Meanwhile, I'll have to ask you to stop talking to Sally about the body, and how people go to the bathroom. I think it makes her nervous."

Ken and Eddie liked to work with clay. They rolled some snakes, modeled some exaggerated, droopy penises, threw some lumps of clay at each other, then they settled down to make clay models of "Gigantor," their favorite television robot-monster. I said Gigantor was make-believe. They said he was real. "Everything on TV is real," Ken said. "We see it, don't we? How could it not be real if we see it?"

Children are born metaphysicians, as well as problem-solvers. I wasn't ready that day to debate the reliability of the senses, or the nature of objective reality, or what was ideal and what was essence, but I knew Gigantor wasn't real. I told Ken and Eddie that Gigantor was an animated cartoon, a series of drawings from some man or woman's imagination. They wouldn't believe me. Ken laughed when I said that robots were just machines made out of metal, like old tomato cans, and that they had no brains as people did. I told him robots could solve simple problems because people built them to do it.

ME (*to Ken, as he flew his clay Gigantor for the fifth consecutive day*): Does Gigantor have a brain?

KEN: Yes, we saw the X-rays!

I was thinking about how to answer that when Ken said, "Steve, I saw you over there at the juice table, eating a lot of cookies just now. Were you hungry or were you just frightened?

Ken was right. I told him I probably was feeling frightened about something, but couldn't think of what it was. Then Ken asked "How come you didn't hit, then?"

There were two other physiological signs of fear that I saw: thumb sucking, and sour, or 'bad,' breath. Adults tend to think that children with such problems are either dirty or careless. We've been taught to fear offending others with our bodily odors, which arise not only from not bathing, but from fear and anxiety. If we offend, it means that people will think we are bad, and we will have no friends. We will ultimately be alone, isolated. I found that when children were particularly frightened, their breath smelled unpleasant, probably because their fear made it difficult for them to completely digest their food.

I asked Denah Harris why she thought five- and six-year-olds sucked their thumbs. I could understand it when they were hungry and tired, but why did they do it when they were frightened?

When babies are frightened by a dream or a loud noise, she explained, the only way they have to communicate is by crying. Fear is complex, and could have many causes. A mother, having no way of knowing why the baby is afraid, tries to meet the needs she is aware of. If he is wet, she changes him. Is there a pin sticking him? Are his clothes binding him? Is he in an uncomfortable position? Can he breathe all right? If the answer to these questions is no, the assumption is that the baby is hungry, and into the mouth goes a bottle, a breast, or some other kind of food. And if, over the years, the automatic and unconscious response to his fear is food, then, as the child gets older, whenever he is frightened, he will eat, because he has learned this as a primary response to fear. Thus, he would eventually learn to deny fear. Maybe this is why so many people smoke and drink too much, and eat more than their bodies need.

One day on the playground, Sally ran up to us, crying. Very gently, Annie asked, "What happened, Sally?" (The children rarely showed or expressed concern for each other when they were hurt or frightened. They would stand around the troubled child, staring, but rarely tried to help. Among those who did, it was almost invariably the girls who reached out to troubled children, whether they were boys or girls. I wondered if it was because they identified with their mothers, and it is women whom the culture has designated as the comforters. They are "allowed" to show solicitude; men are not.)

Sally sobbed, too upset to catch her breath. Sarah answered for her. "Dwayne punched her!"

"My stomach hurts," Sally finally managed to say between sobs. I asked her if Dwayne had punched her in the stomach. Sobbing, she answered, "No, in the arm!"

After I comforted her and she was calmer, I said, "Sally, I'm sorry that Dwayne hurt you. Marilyn is going to talk to him about it. I'm sure he feels badly, too. Let's you and I look at the body book and see about your stomach. Sometimes, when we're frightened, our brains make our stomachs manufacture too much of a bitter juice called acid."

I showed Sally a picture of the digestive system, pointed out the intestines, and told her she might have gas there; that it was a common reaction to being anxious and frightened. I hoped that she and the other children would begin to see a relationship between their fear and the symptoms they got in connection with it. In something as simple as a cut finger, they began to understand a cause-and-effect connection between an explanation of the physiology and a diminishing of the fear. Other situations were more complicated, but if fear caused minor symptoms and exacerbated them, might it not cause major ones as well?

I gave children two kinds of information to counteract their two most prevalent fears. These were: first, that they were bad, and would die from various kinds of punishment for being bad, including illness, accidents, spankings, and partial or total exclusion by parents, friends, and teachers; and second, that they (and others) acted in ways that were categorized as bad because people were born that way, and *wanted* to hurt each other.

The first type of information I provided was physiological. Over and over, I would repeat that human beings are problem-solvers because our bodies and brains have certain inborn functions and potentials. One potential that all human beings have is the ability to solve very complicated problems; this is because our brains are highly developed, and the function of the human cortex is to solve problems.

Next, I explained destructive behavior, their own and other people's, in a nonmoral way, which I hoped would reduce their fears of themselves and others as "bad" or evil. I offered them an alternative to the idea they had been brought up with, that human beings are born good and evil and die for their "sins."

The children also needed to understand that destructive behavior hurts. One day, for example, Mike asked me why it hurt to get hit in the testicles. I drew a picture of a nude man, and explained how nerves connect the testicles to the brain; how a nerve impulse travels, and how all men and boys feel the same sensation of pain if they are hit in the testicles. Some of the children didn't believe that adults felt pain because they never saw us cry. They laughed in disbelief when I told them that I cried sometimes, and so did their parents.

"Only babies cry," Eddie yelled. "I never cry. I'm not afraid of nothing!"

Young children often don't believe that others experience pain. Once, in a junior high school, I stopped four boys from stomping another boy their own age. The victim shrieked in terror, and blood streamed from his nose and mouth.

"How could you do this?" I yelled. "Couldn't you see how much you were hurting him?"

"We weren't hurting him," one of the attackers said, his face as blank as a robot, totally devoid of empathy. "If it hurt him, we would have stopped."

Bomber pilots must experience this kind of denial, and people at prize fights, yelling for "their" fighter to beat his opponent. They suspend all identification with the opponent as a human being. In a sense they have to deny his pain; if they acknowledged it, they would feel it, and it's difficult to yell for blood if you know it's your own.

Both Eddie and Ken hit me in the testicles several times. Once, without warning, Eddie hit me so hard that I dropped to my knees with tears in my eyes. Both of them used to threaten me, and each other, "You better watch out. I'm going to hit you right in the dick!"

The threat worked. I became anxious, and was tempted to say, as if to an adult, "You do, and I'll punch you right in the nose!" This was the answer they feared to one of the questions they were asking. "Will you punish me if I threaten or hit you?" They were also asking why people hurt each other in that way, and what happens to the body when one gets hit in the testicles.

I learned to be ready to protect my groin by pulling my hips back and putting one hand in front of me when there was any sudden movement in that area. The children's hitting, hugging, pushing, and squeezing level was at just that height. I don't remember any of the girls threatening to hit me (or the boys) in the testicles, but Melba threatened to "cut off your heinie and cook it up," and a few children threatened to cut off their classmates' heads, as well as mine.

I explained the physiology of the testicles to the children so they would know their function, utility, strength, *and* their vulnerability to pain. I finished explaining how nerve impulses traveled after a blow, from the testicles to the brain and back, and went to get one of the body books.

"Wait a minute," Mike said, "You don't need that." With a look of great seriousness, standing almost at attention, he pulled down his pants and his underwear, and stood pointing at his testicles.

"Here they are," he said, "and this is what they look like." A few boys and girls bent over solemnly to examine him.

"Where's the nerves?" Caroline asked.

"Inside," Mike said.

Ken ran by and slapped Mike on the buttocks. "I see your heinie!" he yelled.

Mike's eyes filled with tears. Without a word, he slowly pulled his pants up and walked away, shaking his head.

Later that day, Mike was sitting on a hot radiator. Without

thinking how literally most children interpret everything adults say, and hoping to cheer him up, I smiled and said, "You'll cook your behind if you sit there too long." Mike laughed, but Eddie heard me, and repeated, over and over, "He'll cook his ass, he'll cook his ass!"

"I was only joking, Eddie," I said. "That radiator isn't nearly hot enough to cook anything. When there's enough heat to really cook something, the fibers break down from being heated." I explained what happened to the fibers in a green bean, and in a hamburger, when they were cooked.

"That's very interesting," Eddie said, "but Mike is burning his uterus!"

Norel, who was four, needed physiological information more than any child I worked with. His teacher said Norel didn't seem to know whether he was a boy or a girl. When she asked him which he was, he shrugged. For weeks, he walked around school in a long, blond Dynel wig, and a dress, which he got from the dress-up corner in his class room. One day, still wearing his costume, he bumped into me on the stairs.

ME: Hi, Norel. What are you dressed up as?

NOREL (*raising his eyebrows and pouting coyly*): What, honey?

ME: Why are you wearing a wig and a dress?

NOREL: Watch your mouth, honey!

ME: Norel, you can wear any costume you want, but you've been wearing that wig and dress for weeks.

NOREL: They my clothes.

ME: Do you wear clothes like that at home, ever?

NOREL: What you see is what you get!

[So that was it! Norel was understudying Flip Wilson, who wore women's clothes every week on television, and impersonated a sardonic black woman named Geraldine.]

ME: Are you pretending to be Geraldine, Norel?

NOREL: I *am* Geraldine, honey!

ME: I know it must be confusing for you to see Flip Wilson dress as a man and a woman. Do you know whether Flip is a man or a woman?

NOREL: No.

ME: What about you. Are you a boy or a girl?

NOREL: I don't know.

ME (*gently*): Don't you know you're a boy? [Norel shook his head slowly.] Do you know the difference between a boy and a girl?

NOREL: No.

I told Norel about penises, testicles, vaginas, and uteruses: who had them, and what their functions were. I explained that boys and girls were almost exactly the same, could do all the same things, that their brains and ability to think was the same, and the main difference between them was their sex organs and their urogenital systems.

I asked him if he knew what a penis was. He said no. I pointed to his, and to mine, and said, "Men have them. That's what we wee-wee with. Another word for that is 'urinate.'" He giggled. "My mother and aunt said you ain't never supposed to talk about that. Never. They are bad words!"

"Maybe your mother doesn't know that you need to learn about your body. Maybe we can talk to her about that."

"I hope so, honey."

Norel's teacher said he could visit our class while the children and I took apart and put together The Visible Man. Norel sat off to the side, looking very small, the blond wig in his lap, the dress almost covering his shoes. Fascinated, he moved closer to examine The Visible Woman's uterus, the fetus, and The Visible Man's penis. When it was time for Norel to return to his class, he motioned for me to bend down. "Y'all do this every day?" he whispered in my ear.

"Most days."

"All right, then, I'll be back. You hear?"

"Sure," I said, "you can come whenever you want to . . ."

I couldn't answer all of Norel's questions about boys and girls, men and women, and I didn't try to. Norel had many questions that this one experience could only begin to answer, but he came back a few days later, without the wig and the dress.

One winter evening at a parents' meeting, Alan's father said he had a bone to pick with me.

"You and your physiology," he said, smiling. "The other day, Alan and I went to make a snowman in the park; just a regular everyday snowman like my father used to make with me. I rolled a little ball for the head, and a big ball for the body. I had a carrot in my pocket, and I figured all I needed was a few pieces of coal for the eyes and the buttons. All of a sudden, Alan said, 'Wait a minute, Daddy! That's not a *real* snowman!'

" 'What do you mean, it's not a *real* snowman?!'

" 'If it's real, where's the skeleton, veins, arteries, and nerves?' "

Like many children, Eddie would ask a question, and, without waiting for an answer, go on to five or six more. One day, for example, it went this way:

EDDIE: Hey, would you crack my head open and see what my brain looks like?

ME: No, of course not.

EDDIE: Why not?

ME: Because, first, I wouldn't want to hurt you, and that would hurt plenty. Second, I can look at a picture in a book, or at a model of a brain, and see what it looks like. People's brains look very much alike. Besides, if I cracked your head open, it wouldn't be so simple to put it back together. You need to be an expert.

EDDIE: Would I die?

ME: Probably, but I wouldn't do it.

EDDIE: Is there blood in there?

ME: Yes, if . . .

EDDIE (*changing the subject quickly*): Do you peepee inside a lady to make a baby?

ME: No.

EDDIE: Well, what do you do?

ME: When a boy gets to be twelve or thirteen, sometimes a little older, a liquid, called semen, can come out of his penis. It's thicker than water, and it has little tiny invisible things in it called sperms.

EDDIE: You mean you can't pee-pee anymore when you're a man!?

ME: Yes, you still urinate, because that's how you get rid of the liquid waste in your body.

EDDIE: Is sperm like doodie?

ME: No it's very different from doodie. The sperm is made inside a male's testicles. . . . You know what I mean by male?

EDDIE: A letter?

ME: No, that's the other kind of mail. *M-a-i-l* is letters, and *m-a-l-e* is a way of saying boys and men. Now, do you know what testicles are?

EDDIE (*laughing*): Balls!

ME: Right. The sperm is in the semen. It comes up from the testicles into the penis. When a man puts his penis into a woman's vagina, the sperm travels through the penis, into the vagina, and up into the uterus, where the woman has a very tiny egg . . . you can hardly see it . . .

EDDIE: Hold it. I don't think I want to do that.

ME: Do what?

EDDIE: You know, put my penis in a woman's vagina. It sounds messy.

ME: Maybe you'll change your mind later on. Then you'll need this information.

EDDIE: I'll give you a call if I do. Finish about the baby.

ME: O.K. The sperm touches the egg, joins with it, and the egg begins to grow inside the uterus.

EDDIE: What's a uterus?

ME: It's the place where the baby grows inside a woman. I'll show you a picture of it.

EDDIE: Did you know the baby's head comes out of the vagina first?

ME: Usually it does, but sometimes the legs do.

EDDIE: O.K., Steve. That's all for today. I'll teach you some more tomorrow.

Eddie kissed me shyly on the cheek, hit me on the arm, and ran down the stairs singing the song he made up, the one I called "Eddie's Blues": "When your brain dies, you die, . . . and that ain't good!"

6

Children's Games: Acting Out Taboo Questions

In the summer the children loved to go to the playground and run under the sprinkler. All year round, they used the jungle gym, swings, seesaws, and the sandbox. In the classroom they enjoyed board games, puzzles, and arts and crafts. Since the school had a terrarium, an aquarium, turtles, gerbils, and rabbits, there was plenty to do and see, but when the children weren't involved in a structured activity, they made up games.

The girls usually played house and hospital. The boys played games about monsters, cops and robbers, cowboys and Indians, astronauts, and wild animals. The girls rarely volunteered to play with them; more often they were drafted when the boys captured them and put them in some kind of prison. Both boys and girls usually played games in which someone was in jeopardy or imperiled by death; their interest in games involving death as a climax was almost obsessive. Over and over again, they were asking, "Why do people punish, hurt, and lock each other up?" Not surprisingly, when I asked them about their death fears, after seeing them act out these questions in their games, the children often withdrew, or tried to divert me. Children learn these strategies from adults, when they ask questions about death.

In death games, someone always has to be "It." In "Hot Pot," a game I described in Chapter 1, the girls were It because they are ostensibly weaker. The class learned the game from Marky, who learned it somewhere else—whether from other children or from a movie or television program is not important. What is crucial is to realize that the theme of imprisonment and punishment by death, which is dramatized in the game, runs through our entire culture. Children, by playing the games they do, implore us to answer their questions about these themes; questions which neither they nor we are consciously aware they are asking, and which they are not allowed to ask verbally, and we are not allowed to answer.

"Gigantor" is a cartoon series about a giant metal robot who is controlled by a young boy. The children identified with young Jimmy, who could summon Gigantor at any time, to smash the robots and monsters developed by the "bad guys." This tarnished but sturdy plot existed even before David and Goliath. We have already noted that most five- and six-year-olds believed that these cartoon characters were real; that anything they saw on television was real because they saw it.

I acted out some of the roles they saw on television; cowboy, caveman, judge, and doctor. To be more convincing, I should have used costumes, and asked Marilyn to dramatize some women's roles. (A closed-circuit television system would be an even better way to demonstrate the difference between acting and reality; the children could see themselves on film moments after they acted out a role.) Since there were no costumes or cameras, my improvisation had to do, and at least the children could see how actors pretend to be many people, play many roles. The child's willingness to suspend disbelief, to be drawn into the dramatization of reality problems as questions of good and evil, is constantly abused in children's storybooks, theater, and television. Young children will believe almost anything, so we tell them anything. We tell them "make-believe" stories which confuse their sense of reality, because we were told such stories, and taught that we liked to hear them.

Some children asked, "If Gigantor isn't real, how does he do all those things?" I showed them how an animated cartoon is made, and helped them to draw their own cartoon sequences, which they pulled rapidly back and forth in front of their eyes until the separate drawings began to look as if they were moving. We also made books out of a series of cartoons they drew, which they could flip rapidly, "animating" the drawings.

"Why do grownups make up stories to scare kids, if they aren't real?" Terry asked.

"Because when those grownups were little, people scared them with stories and told them they *liked* being scared. Now *they're* making up stories, as a way of asking why people scared them when they were little. But those stories scare other people's children, and even their own," I explained.

"That's mean!" Annie said.

"They don't do it to be mean," I insisted. "They do it because they don't know that children don't like to be frightened. They think they're being nice to kids."

Scott suddenly rose up on his toes, his eyes went blank, and he put his hands out in front of him stiffly.

"I am a monster," he said, "I am Frankenstein!"

He stalked Annette, who ran away, shrieking. Sometimes the child whom the monster stalked appeared to enjoy the game, but not this time—Annette was pale and frightened.

I said to Scott, "You know, I think that frightens Annette."

"Does that frighten you?" he asked her.

"Yes, it does. Stop doing it." (I had expected Annette to deny fear, but she didn't.)

A few minutes later, when all the children were gathered in the playground, Annette said to them, "I have a message for the boys. Don't play monster and chase the girls. It frightens us." At the end of the day, Annette told me, "I think the boys understood. They're not chasing the girls." But the next day they were back at it, yelling, "Kill them, get them, put them in the hot pot!"

The next day, Scott jumped on me from the jungle gym, yelling, "I am Batman!" The "Batman" TV serials were being rerun weekday afternoons after school, and most of the boys watched the programs and acted out the adventures in school.

As I unwrapped his arms from around my throat I asked him not to jump on me: "It hurts. Let's talk, instead of wrestling."

Scott tried to wrestle with me every day. He told me he and his father wrestled every night. He said they never talked to each other, except when his father was mad, and yelled at him.

SCOTT: My father always wrestles with me. It's fun, and Batman wrestles with everyone. He punches them, too!

ME: I know. I've seen the program. Batman is trying to solve problems by punishing people he thinks are bad. You can't solve any problems or learn anything by punching people, but it is fun to wrestle sometimes.

SCOTT: You said Batman isn't real.

ME: That's right, he isn't. It's a man, an actor, pretending to be someone called Batman, but people really can and do hurt each other the way the actor who is playing Batman is doing. . . . Remember when we talked about how people who pretend in stories are called actors?"

While Scott thought about this, Arthur came over.

"My father is the real Batman," he said, "but he doesn't wear his cape when he comes here."

Arthur's intervention was typical of the difficulty of trying to answer one child's questions in a room filled with twenty-four alert, vital children with questions of their own.

SCOTT: My daddy is just plain daddy.

BILLY (*who wandered over*): My grandfather died, and came back to life. My cousin told me.

I wanted to respond to the crucial question within Billy's statement, but the momentum of the group which spontaneously developed, swept us on. Often, when we began to discuss the meaning of some games the children were playing, a child made a statement or raised a question about death. I tried to pick up on their statements later, when we could work alone.

ARTHUR: I know my father is the real Batman, because he says he has a lot of friends who are crooks.

(This conversation, like many we had, took its own direction. I include it as an example of the difficulty in holding onto the thread of one conversation with a group of young children.)

One afternoon, I came upon three boys and a girl lying motionless on the floor. "This boy is dead," the girl said. "He got shot by an Indian." The other children dragged the "dead" child into the bathroom.

"Don't put me in the bathroom, guys!" the "dead" man screamed. "I don't want to be alone in there in the dark!" The three children carrying him said they were Superman, Batman, and Supergirl.

"This is what we do to bad people, lock 'em up in a dark room, but we'll be nice to you this time." She patted the boy on the back. "Feel better?" she asked. She told me she was a nurse, and that nurses "help dead people get better."

She lay down, closed her eyes for a moment, then jumped up, again Supergirl: "I better kill him. Lie down, Batman! Batman lie down."

Then, alarmed; "Batman, Batman, are you all right?!" Batman got up.

"I'm alive again," he said.

As they played, they yelled, "Pow! Pow! ," the word that appeared in the Batman serial, superimposed as pop-art print over the live characters. In the melee following the game, all the children kicked each other, Supergirl kicked me, and everyone yelled, "Pow! Pow!"

They continued to take turns playing dead. The roles were undifferentiated, except that none of the boys wanted to be Supergirl, whereas the girls wanted to be Superman, Batman, or Robin. Besides Supergirl, Robin was the least popular role, probably because he is the youngest, the weakest, the most vulnerable, and the least invincible. In addition to the "pow!'s," all they said was, "You're dead. I killed you!"

It was apparent from these games that it was more desirable, safer, to be a male than a female. It was also clear that hitting, killing, and dying were what the children remembered from the programs, and that they thought death was both a punishment and a temporary sleep.

Gun play wasn't banned in Marilyn's classroom, but guns were, so the children used blocks as guns, or modeled them out of clay. Many nursery school teachers don't permit children to bring guns or war toys to school since they think these toys increase tension in a classroom. But banning guns doesn't eliminate gun play. Children use their imaginations to simulate weapons, and continue to act out questions about death and killing.

Although even three- and four-year-olds acted out games of death and dying, there was much less war, gun, and monster play among them than among five- and six-year-olds.

As children get older, they see and experience more violence, and feel more threatened by the irrational behavior around them. Increasingly exposed to judgments about who is good and bad, their questions as to what is good and bad behavior become more urgent. Children test adults and each other to learn what punishment results from disobeying, and whether death is the ultimate punishment for being bad.

For weeks, I had tried to get Eddie and Ken to be friends. At first, they competed for my attention. They fought with each other and with the other children. Both of them hit me if they thought I was too attentive to the other. I told them that I cared about them equally, that if I spent time with one, it didn't mean I liked the other one less, but that I was helping them to learn to be friends with each other when I wasn't there. My explanation didn't help.

One day, in the playground, Ken broke up a game I was playing with another child. I asked him to put his question in words. He couldn't.

"You don't have to do that to get me to talk to you. Just ask me," I said. Ken tried to get on my lap and kiss me. When Eddie saw him, he tried to do the same thing. Since I'd seen them playing together a few minutes earlier, I asked them if they were problem-solving. They said they were, and went off together to the other side of the playground.

I soon realized that their idea of cooperative problem-solving was ganging up on other children. It was like television; they made a coalition, a conspiracy, proclaimed themselves the good guys, designated some bad guys, and found someone else to "get," which means to punish. They called their game "The Monsters Kill the Children."

Very often, children's idea of playing together is to gang up, to tease, torment, or fight other children. Their model for cooperation, on television, in the movies, and in children's stories (in the neighborhood, and often at home) is to find allies, then work together with them to overwhelm or beat an adversary. Outside of the sandbox, the children rarely worked together to create something. Instead they would break something or beat someone. Perhaps this pervasive competition I saw in nursery schools exists partly because television provides visual models for violence; and the news, which children watch, is full of war. I don't know whether children's games are more violent than they used to be, but the children I saw, in and out of the classrooms, played primarily violent games.

One day in music class, the children were learning "The Spider and the Fly." The music teacher asked if anyone knew how spiders walked.

EDDIE (*as he raised his hand*): My mother says spiders kill people . . . do they? [The music teacher didn't answer.] I saw a spider. I stepped on it.

MUSIC TEACHER: Eddie, please be quiet. We're learning a song now.

EDDIE: I put a hole in its back. I crushed him everywhere. I killed him. I took my father's gun and killed him, and then I took my toy machine gun. I killed him, but he came back to life.

MUSIC TEACHER: I see. We're going to act out "The Spider and the Fly." Would you like to be the spider, Eddie?

EDDIE: Yes, I'm a spider.

OTHER CHILDREN: Can I be the fly?

I empathized with the music teacher. Eddie was asking questions about whether spiders were a threat to his life, about killing, about the nature of death (" . . . I killed him, but he came back to life."); about the tormenting fears which prevented him from concentrating on music, or on any other learning.

The music teacher wasn't prepared to answer him, even if she had recognized his fantasies as questions. Her job was to teach music, and Eddie was distracting the class with his "morbid fantasies." She hoped to divert him by asking him to be the spider, but Spider Eddie ran hysterically around the room, biting the other children and yelling, "You're dead. I killed you!"

The other children imitated his fear, and began running around the room, shrieking and biting each other. The music lesson was over.

Perhaps a more experienced teacher could have diverted Eddie, but unless his questions about spiders and death were answered, eventually he would act them out, and teach them to the other children, if they didn't already know them.

One day, Dwayne suddenly fell down in the playground and lay motionless. After a few seconds he jumped up, stamped on a bug, and lay down again.

DWAYNE: I killed that roach, now I'm dead, too!

ANNIE AND EVELYN (*who were watching*): Ooooh, goody!

EVELYN: We'll have to find the ambulance for him. Dwayne, open your mouth. I'll give you some medicine. In three days you'll be better.

ME: What are you playing, Dwayne?

DWAYNE: I'm playing sleep.

EVELYN: He's playing hospital.

ANNIE: He's playing dead. [The girls woke him up.]

DWAYNE (*as he got up*): I'm upset today. I'm sad at everyone. [Dwayne had a hard time making friends, mainly because he so often hit the other children. His babysitter and housekeeper both spanked him. His mother told me she hired help who would do as she told them.] I didn't have any breakfast this morning, and I didn't see my mommy. There's a lion on "Sesame Street" who bites people's heads off. That's why I'm upset.

Dwayne acted out his questions about death with the girls. His first question, when he killed the roach, was "Do you die for killing?" Then he acted out his question about the difference between death and sleep, which is a very common question among children. (They often asked, "Are dead people sleeping?") Dwayne might also have been asking whether his mommy still cared about him, since she didn't come to see him before she left for work, and didn't see that he got his breakfast. His last question was, "Do lions kill people by biting their heads off?"

I told Dwayne I thought that, by lying down and playing dead after he killed the roach, he was asking whether death was a punishment for killing any living thing.

"After all," I told him, "there is functional and nonfunctional killing. Roaches don't have brains and can't think, so we can't ask them not to spread germs and dirt, and expect them to be able to cooperate with us. It is functional to kill roaches and bugs that destroy plant and animal life, because we can't teach them not to be destructive. It's also functional to kill cows, goats, sheep, rabbits, fish and some other animals, for food, and for clothing, but it's never functional to kill human beings because we can solve problems, or to kill any fish, insect, or animal for sport.

"Sometimes men kill animals in order to experiment on them, to increase what we know about how their bodies work, so we can help other animals and human beings. Sometimes animals kill humans, for food or out of fear."

Dwayne seemed satisfied, but I wondered if this wasn't functional killing, too. We still need a better explanation, ecologically and rationally. Many people think it's never functional to kill any living animal, for any reason; that all living things have equal right to the earth. It's a question that can't be resolved here. Many children become vegetarians when they learn that the hot dogs and hamburgers they love are made from dead animals, killed for their flesh.

I went on to explain to Dwayne that death was not like sleep, even though dead bodies looked something like living people asleep. If you watch a sleeping person closely, you will see him move in his sleep, see him breathe, see his eyelids flutter. Dead bodies can't move or breathe, because the part of the body that makes everything work, the brain, has stopped working forever, and can never work again. A sleeping person isn't dead, I told Dwayne, and a dead person isn't sleeping.

He thought about what I said. "What about the lions?" he asked. "Do they bite people's head off?"

"I'm sure it must have happened a very few times, but not often, unless people put their heads in the lion's mouth. People aren't lion food. Lions eat zebras and deer, and animals like that. If they got very hungry, and had nothing else to eat, they might eat a person."

Dwayne suddenly looked worried.

"But, you're not going to be where there are any hungry lions, anyway."

He smiled with relief.

"Human beings kill many lions. Lions hardly ever kill human beings," I went on.

"Lions are bad," Dwayne argued. "They should be killed."

"I don't think so."

"I'm bad," Dwayne confessed. "I should be killed."

"I don't think so," I repeated.

"I'm glad," Dwayne said, running to join the other children.

On the playground that afternoon, Teddy raced around screaming, "A ghost, a ghost!" Danny was the ghost. He chased Teddy, his head lolling, his eyes unfocused, his arms flapping, and his mouth hanging open, drooling. The other children shrieked loudly, and I had to hold Teddy on my lap.

His body shook and he was weeping as I explained that there were no ghosts.

"I see big giant ghosts, big lion monsters," Teddy said.

"Where?"

"On TV. Casper the Ghost."

The other children, who gathered around Teddy and me, began to play ghost. Marilyn came over to see why they were screaming so loud.

MARILYN: What are you doing, kids?

MINDY: We're pretending we're ghosts!

MARILYN: Why?

MINDY: We like it.

ERIC: No, we don't like it! We want to know about them . . .

TEDDY: We're monsters . . .

ROBERT (*making a monster face at me*): I am a terrible monster!

ME: Did you see that on television?

ROBERT: No, in a dream, but I wasn't afraid.

ME: I didn't say you were afraid, but maybe I could help you, anyway . . .

ROBERT: I said I *wasn't* afraid!

ME: O.K.

The children began to go "Bang! Bang!" and the ghost game became Cops and Robbers. Nevertheless, the questions about death and punishment were consistently present. Eric even managed to say, "We want to know about ghosts," but that was unusual. More often, children acted out the questions in games.

When they get a few years older, these games become inappropriate for children, and their questions begin to take different forms. Sports, dating, social competition for popularity, and the battle of the sexes are all later stages of asking questions in the evolution of children's games. The object of all these games people play is to be in the good category, the safe category, to compete to be on top, so as not to be on the bottom, not to be unpopular or bad; to be one up, not one down: To win. These games are forms of war. Too soon, the boys go off to fight in real wars, become real cops and robbers, while the girls, handmaidens to the warriors, wait for their return.

Teddy and Robert played a shooting game, using red and blue measuring rods as guns. They shot at Evelyn and Annie, who shot back from behind a bookcase. Marilyn broke up the game, and got them back to work without talking to them about their game, although both boys were unusually tense and excited.

After class, I asked Marilyn why she hadn't dealt with the children's unspoken questions. She explained that she had broken up the game not so much because shooting games were frightening—which they were—but because Teddy and Robert took the rods they used as guns from another child who was using them to measure something. She argued that children needed answers to questions about each other's rights as well as to the questions they were acting out.

Annie and Evelyn were playing hospital.

"I am the nurse," Annie said, "and this (pointing to a piece of felt-covered plywood) is what you carry dead people on." Dwayne, Beth, and Teddy took turns playing dead.

Suddenly, Dwayne hit Teddy and Beth with the "stretcher." "I'll make you dead!" he yelled.

"Stop that, Dwayne," Annie said. "We need a dead person, but not one of us."

"What will you do with the dead person?" I asked.

"Take them to the hospital. . . . Oh," she said, "there's Beth. She could be the dead one."

"Not me," said Beth. "I'm not dead, because I have a brain." Dwayne, Annie, and Evelyn immediately turned and shot her.

"Bang! Now you're dead!"

"You can't kill me. My brain is working." (Beth was willing

to try out new information about physiology, perhaps because both of her parents were biologists.)

I made a note to clarify a misconception she might have had, that a functioning brain meant one wouldn't die; that it was a talisman against death. Teddy suddenly fell down. "I'm dead again," he said.

Dwayne started to "bury Teddy alive" by rolling him up in a mat. Teddy shrieked with terror. I told Dwayne to unroll him, and helped him to do it quickly.

Soon the "stretcher" became the roof of a house. The death game abated, and the children became calm. Five minutes later, at the juice table, Teddy said, "I'm angry with Dwayne, Annie, and all of the children. I'm not coming back to this school."

ME: Are you afraid about the game all of you were playing?

TEDDY: Yes. I was afraid they'd make me dead. [I lifted Teddy on to my lap, and held him gently.]

ME: They were afraid, too. They won't make you dead or hurt you. They were just playing a game to learn what happens when you die. They have questions about what death is, just like you do. In the game, they were asking questions, like you were. I know you're frightened, and that *was* a scary game.

The other children sat around us, listening quietly as they drank their juice.

A few days later, Teddy, Dwayne and I were sitting together, drawing.

TEDDY: Let's play dead.

ME: Why do you want to play dead?

TEDDY: Policemen make robbers dead, and they're sad. Robbers make policemen dead, and they're sad.

ME: That's true. Do you want to talk about why people make each other dead?

TEDDY: No, I don't like it! You're not supposed to talk about it!

Only three, Teddy had already learned that talking about death was taboo. Upset, he threw a puzzle down hard, screamed, and made animal noises. I dropped the subject, but it was clear to me what his fear was.

In the class we gradually explored death as a biological process, and the children learned that the brain controlled the functioning of the entire body. They learned that death occurred when the brain stopped functioning, and then a person could no longer feel or experience anything. Above all I emphasized that death was not a punishment. Society does not usually allow children to talk about death, but they are allowed to play games which dramatize it, and they do, over and over again. I continually explained to them, though, that their bodies were beautiful organizations of energy, tremendously strong, and capable of repairing themselves.

Children played other games which dramatized their need for information about themselves and the world around them. Boys and girls often went into the bathroom and played Doctor, Nurse, Hospital, and You Show Me Yours, I'll Show You Mine—probably the most forbidden yet educational physiology game of all. They examined each other's genitals with great curiosity. Of course, they stopped as soon as an adult entered, even though toilets in many classrooms were "open"—that is, both boys and girls used them. When there were two commodes in one bathroom, it wasn't unusual to see a boy and a girl sitting next to each other, chatting calmly. But the children had already learned that exploring genitals, theirs or others, was taboo, as was asking questions about how genitals function. So, as children always have, they played You Show Me Yours when no adults were around.

I hope they won't *have* to go on playing this game or more urgent games as their only way of getting the information they need. If we hear the questions within the games they play, we can begin to answer them, and then encourage them to discover the answers for themselves.

7

Religion: Does God Punish Little Kids for Being Bad?

Sandra's father was a fundamentalist minister. She was a friendly, outgoing child, but her eyes were filled with fear, and her muscles were hard with the isometrics of tension. Her movements were as jerky as those of a cartoon character, and she constantly threatened her classmates with a wide range of violent deaths. Some idea of her fearful obsessions can be gained from this conversation during a fight she had one day with Eddie:

SANDRA: I'm going to get you for that, Eddie. You ripped up my stuff. I'm going to knock your head into the ground where the devil will eat it and burn it up!

[Eddie also had some thoughts about hell. His mother read him Bible stories every night, from which he quoted long passages from memory.]

EDDIE: I'll chop off your fingers and take them to the Sea of Galilee. Sharks will eat them there, and the archangel will come in fiery robes, and cut off your head with a sword!

SANDRA: I'll screw off your head with a gas decoder. Maybe I'll get the devil to do it. If that doesn't kill you, I'll get my dog on you. He has bad breath from eating canned dog food, and you'll go to hell for sure.

EDDIE: I'll pound some thorns in your face.

SANDRA: I'm not afraid of anything. I'm brave and I never cry. [Her eyes fill with tears as her face tenses.] If monsters try to scare me on TV, I get a monster mask. I put it on and scare the monster.

A few minutes later, as the class sat down to hear a story, Sandra began to yell, and ran around the room as if something was after her, constantly looking back over her shoulder. I caught her as she ran by, and pulled her on to my lap.

ME: Are you frightened, Sandra? I heard you and Eddie talking—

SANDRA: Eddie is going to send me to hell and cut my head off!

ME: No one can send you to hell, there's no such place.

SANDRA: Yes there is, my father said so. He said the devil sends for you if you're bad.

ME: What do you think?

SANDRA: I think he's right. What do *you* think?

ME: I don't think so.

SANDRA: Why not?

ME: Because I don't think there's any such place as hell.

SANDRA: What about heaven?

ME: I don't think there's a heaven either.

SANDRA: Where does God live, then?

ME: A lot of people think there's a God. I don't—

SANDRA (*shouting*): I'm telling my father you said that!

ME: You know, Sandra, different people think different things about heaven and hell. Some people think they exist, and some don't. Everyone in the world doesn't think the same way.

Parents who had no objections to their children learning about psysiology, excretion, and sex, were very reluctant for me to explore religion with their children. The taboos against discussing death and religion were the strongest I encountered. Realizing the difficulties this presented not only for me, but for the children and their parents as well, I deliberately avoided asking children about God, and what they thought about life after death, because these questions elicited further questions from them. When that happened, I could either hedge, change the subject, or answer. After stepping gingerly around the topic, I usually answered them because these questions came up over and over again, as a source of wonder, curiosity, and fear.

As I expected, Sandra told her father about our conversation. The next day he phoned to ask me not to discuss religion with his daughter; he would "handle" that area of her education. "My wife and I have no objections to Sandra's learning about physiology, but religion is an area that's out of bounds for school—and for teachers."

"Reverend Gardner, I think there's a misunderstanding. Sandra asked me what I thought about heaven and hell. I wasn't really teaching her religion."

"I didn't say that you were, but if she brings it up again, tell her to ask me. That's my job."

"And if she asks me what I think about God or religion . . ."

"Don't answer her."

"Suppose some other children have questions about religion, and Sandra happens to be listening. That's very likely to happen. What do you suggest I do then?"

"Be resourceful. Tell her to find something else to do. Tell her that her parents don't want her to discuss religion in school."

"If I did that, it would probably make her more curious. She might ask why."

"Let's cross that bridge when we come to it," he said sharply. "Each person's religion is his own business. It just happens that religion is my business. Teaching numbers and letters is yours . . ."

"I'm afraid I don't see it quite that way."

"I'm responsible for raising Sandra, you're not. I don't want to argue with you."

"I'm not arguing with you."

"Good," Reverend Gardner said. "Then I'm going to ask you to stay away from this topic completely. By telling Sandra you don't think there's a God, you are thoroughly undermining our authority."

We'd reached an impasse. The Reverend was adamant, and if he thought it was wrong for me to answer Sandra's questions, and I couldn't convince him otherwise, I didn't want to be his adversary. I hoped Sandra wouldn't bring up any more religious questions.

Sandra had responded well to the idea of problem-solving. She'd pull me to a quiet corner and ask one question after another: "How do they make cartoons on television?", "How do buildings stay up?", "Why do people rob?", and "Does God see everything you do?" A few days after talking with her father, I asked her if she had any questions for me.

SANDRA: Never again! You're nothing but a stinking atheist! You're polluting my mind with a lot of garbage!

ME: What does that mean, Sandra?

SANDRA: It means you don't go to church; now shut up! And you're just using us for guinea pigs. I'm never talking to you again!"

ME: I'm sad to hear you say that. You and I are friends.

SANDRA: We used to be, but no more. You don't believe in God. You are a very bad man!

Our way to the playground led past a five-and-ten-cent store which displayed three-dimensional pictures of Jesus in the window. His expression changed with the viewer's perspective. Two of them were particularly fascinating to

Eddie: one showed Christ wearing a crown of thorns, the other showed him crucified.

"The mean Israelites killed him," Eddie said sadly. "They bled him to death because they were mean. He died for your sins and mine . . ."

I didn't say anything.

"Didn't he?" Eddie put his finger in his nose, gazing up at me.

Another pause.

"Well he did, even though you're not answering me!"

I didn't answer Eddie because I was remembering the first time I heard about Jesus. When I was five, a German woman who said she used to be a nun moved next door. She wore a dark brown habit, and lived alone in a large, somber house on the corner. She supported herself by selling eggs from the chickens she raised in her attic. It was unusual to raise chickens in an attic in suburban Long Island (there were ten or twelve houses on the block), but even more unusual was the life-sized plaster statue of Christ she placed on her front lawn. The six-foot icon had long, golden hair, a soft, peaceful expression, white robes, and a throbbing, red sacred heart which stood out from the robes in bas-relief. The statue's arms stretched out imploringly, the turned up wrists revealing bleeding stigmata. Almost every family on the block was Jewish, so our new neighbor and her statue were most unusual.

My mother used to send me to buy eggs from the woman, whose name I never knew. She told me to call her Sister. As Christmas approached, she told me the story of the birth and crucifixion of Christ. She showed me a finely detailed crèche, and then some icons which, as I remember, showed much blood, and the whites of Christ's eyes, rolled up in anguish. Her voice was very soft, and her manner gentle, but I was frightened by the strangeness of it all, and by the aura of violent death. I remember my hand sweating, holding the egg basket. The sister's German accent (this was in 1943, and I'd been told about the Germans and the Jews), the darkness of the house, its smell of chickens, and the story of this boy who was born in a barn, then later nailed up and left to bleed to death, was terrifying.

The woman told me that the statue on her lawn was of Jesus after he had risen from the dead, after his crucifixion. I had seen its bleeding wrists and heart, and my own heart began to beat wildly. I handed her the money my mother had given me for the eggs, and ran out of the house, leaving a trail of broken eggs across her back yard.

That was the last time I saw the woman, though not the last time I saw the statue. Her house and lawn were on a bend in the road. Drivers coming around the curve couldn't see the statue until they were about fifty feet away. At night, the vision of this life-sized statue in their head lights caused five or six drivers to swerve and crash into a fence across the street. Most of these accidents occurred on weekends, and the police told our neighbors that the victims had been drinking, but after a while the police, or the neighbors, convinced the woman to remove the statue.

Eddie and Ken were playing with monster-robots they'd modeled out of clay. It was the television robot, Gigantor, again, and they agreed on his invincibility. "Nothing could kill him, nothing could hurt him," Eddie said.

"Yeah," Ken agreed, "he's bigger and stronger than the guy who lives in the sky."

"Whom do you mean?" I asked.

"God!" they yelled together.

"Who told you that?"

"About Guard, you mean?" Ken asked.

"His name isn't Guard, dummy," Eddie said. "It's God."

"Uh-uh, it's Guard, cause he guards you. He's so strong, nothing could hurt him. Like me." Ken flexed his biceps.

As children discover death, they develop an increasing concern with omnipotence and invincibility. They've heard that God, as well as Superman, Batman, and the rest of the superheroes, has both of these characteristics. They become very interested in how he uses his superpower, and act out what it would be like to have this power themselves—to be invincible, to transcend their littleness in a world of big people, and to be generals in a world where they are always privates. They try to experience what it would be like not to be afraid to die. When Evelyn told me she had superpowers I learned that she was exploring the ideas of invincibility and why God supposedly punishes people.

ME: What's superpower?

EVELYN: I could kick people and make them dead, like God.

ME: Why would you think of doing that?

EVELYN (*unable to think of an answer*): Oh, I'd take them to the Garden of God and cut them up.

ME: When do you use your superpower?

EVELYN: On special days.

ME: Like which ones?

EVELYN: If someone hits me, I'll kick them in the head. I only make people I don't know dead. Not people I know. I never really tried it [giggling], so I don't know if I could do it. Anyway, the devil eats people—right, Ken?

KEN (*looking up from the clay monster he was making*): Right, but Guard lives above in the sky. Guard and Jesus are even in your stomach.

ME: Why do you say that?

KEN: Because they're everywhere, aren't they? Then they have to be in your stomach. That's somewhere.

Eddie asked if we could go somewhere alone, just the two of us, and solve problems.

ME: What's the problem?

EDDIE. It's my damn grandma. She whips me with a spoon all the time. She says I'm the devil's work. Now, I wanna' ask you something. If I think she's stupid, will God take me back up there?

ME: Did your grandma tell you that?

EDDIE: Damn right she did! She said if I don't do everything right, the devil will get me. What do you think?

ME: First of all, I don't think the devil is real. I think it's just an idea. Maybe, when your grandma was little, the grownups around her told her the same things she's telling you now about the devil. Your grandma wanted answers to questions, just like you do, but when she tried to get the answers she needed—about things like God, the devil, and religion, they told her she was bad, and not to ask any more questions.

EDDIE: How do you know? You weren't there.

ME: That's true, I wasn't, but people have been telling children the same things for years and years, and they still are. People as old as your grandma have said that they were told to keep quiet if they asked questions when they were little. No one told your grandma she was a problem-solver with a brain. We've just recently come to understand this. You know, Eddie, there are certain ideas most people are afraid to talk about. We're told we're bad if we talk about them. Those things are called taboos, and religion is one of them.

EDDIE: Does God hear everything? Will he punish me if I think bad thoughts?

ME: I don't think so. Some people think there's a God, who punishes people, and some people don't.

EDDIE: What do *you* think?

ME: I told you. I don't think there is.

EDDIE: There is, there has to be! If you kick someone, God will take away your legs. [shouting] God told me that! My grandma says there's a God. Who's right?

ME: It's not who's right, Eddie, it's . . .

EDDIE: She's right! You're wrong. You're bad. You're a faggot!

ME: What's a faggot?

EDDIE: I don't know. It means you're bad . . .

ME: I'm not bad, and neither are you. And you know what? Neither is anyone else. If you say or think something about your grandma that you've learned is bad, that's a taboo question you have, and you've learned to be afraid to ask, because people *do* punish you for asking questions which frighten them. Your grandmother really loves you, and she tries hard to help you the best way she knows how. It's hard work to help a child grow.

EDDIE: She makes too many mistakes.

ME: Everybody makes mistakes.

EDDIE: If you make mistakes, you must be stupid. You're stupid!

ME: Is that a question? Are you asking me? If you make mistakes, are you stupid?

EDDIE: Yeah, that's my question.

ME: You're not stupid if you make mistakes. You're learning, or trying to. If you lack information, you might be ignorant, but you're not stupid. Stupid is another way of saying bad; that someone is bad because he doesn't know.

Terry, too, had been given lots of information about religion, but it only provoked questions no one was helping him with. He often talked about God and the devil as he cut out flying monsters and superheroes with a scissors. "What I'm cutting out here is called the devil," he said. "My mommy said the devil lives in hell. When you're weak, Satan—that's the devil's other name—he tells you to do bad things. Now, God told his son Jesus to go into the desert and think about what he's gonna do. Satan said, 'Since you're the son of God, let's see you turn these rocks into bread.'" He put down his scissors and looked at his paper devil. "The evil spirit took Jesus on a tower, but Jesus said, 'Begone, Satan!' Then two of God's angels gave Jesus food and drink."

God and the devil were only two of Terry's obsessions. He lumped them in with flying monsters, werewolves, and ghosts. In fact, he thought about them so much, it was difficult for him to follow any instructions, or even put his coat and shoes on at the end of the day. Most of the other children dressed themselves quickly, but Terry sat with his shoes next to him, asking us if ghosts and the devil killed children who didn't do as they were told.

One day, Terry, Emily, and Ken asked if we could all solve problems together. Terry wanted to tell us about a Bible story comic book he brought to school. We found an empty room, where the three children began to examine the book together.

KEN: Let me see the strong man on the front cover.

TERRY: That's Samson.

KEN: He thinks he's so strong—is he big? Is he a giant?

ME: You started to tell me about Adam and Eve upstairs, Terry. Do you want to talk some more about that?

TERRY: Yes, this is the devil. You see in this picture? The devil is really a snake.

ME: Is that the Garden of Eden?

TERRY: You mean the Garden of Even.

ME: The way I heard it, it was the Garden of Eden.

TERRY: Well, you heard it wrong, but I'll tell you the story anyway. You see, God told Adam and Eve that they could eat from every tree, "but there's one tree you may not eat from," he said, "the tree of knowledge." But the devil whispered, "You won't die—don't listen to him!"

ME: You mean the snake was really a devil?

TERRY: The snake was really *the* devil! And the devil

snake told Adam and Eve, "Eat the apple; your eyes won't close. Your eyes will still be open. Eat it!" So Eve took a bite of it, and gave Adam some. And then when God appeared in the Garden of Even, they were walking around. God saw an apple picked off, and he was mad.

KEN: Why he was mad?

TERRY: 'Cause, see, God didn't want, did *not* want Adam, or nobody, to eat from the tree of knowledge. [Terry's voice began to take on the cadences of a preacher.]

ME: What does the tree of knowledge mean?

TERRY: I don't know. I just know that Eve talked him into eating the apple.

KEN: How does the story end?

TERRY: Well, they were going to turn him into a lump of sugar, but they didn't.

[I thought this might be Terry's version of Sodom and Gomorrah, so I asked him if he was sure that was the ending.]

TERRY: No, how *does* it end?

ME: In the story, God tells Adam and Eve they have to leave the Garden of Eden, the beautiful place where they were living. They had to leave because they didn't obey him. The garden was like a heaven, and Adam and Eve are supposed to be the first man and woman, who could have lived there forever if they did what God told them. What do you think of the story, Emily?

Emily was thoughtful, and hadn't said anything during Terry's version of Adam and Eve. "I don't know if it's true," she said, "but it may be. When the priests make the bread into Jesus' body, *that's* true. Jesus was God *and* human, right Ken?"

Ken didn't answer. He shrugged, and hummed to himself as he looked out of the window.

TERRY (*in his preacher voice*): And Jesus was a man of flesh and blood!

EMILY: Yes, and he was also God. He was God and human, so he could do anything, right?

TERRY: Right, he was the son of God!

EMILY (*nodding*): Jesus said to his disciples, "Wherever you do this, it will become me.

ME: Will become what to his disciples?

EMILY: Me!

ME: What does disciples mean?

EMILY: His disciples were his friends.

ME (*to Ken*): What do you think about that story?

KEN: I don't know. I never heard it before."

TERRY (*yelling*): Everybody is God's children. Everybody!

EMILY: Yes, Jesus took the bread, and he said to his disciples, "Take this, all of you, and eat from it! This is my body!" Then he took the wine, and he said, "Take this wine and drink from it. This is the blood of my body!"

TERRY: Yeccch!

EMILY: It's true. Because when they gave it to me once, it didn't taste like bread, it really didn't.

TERRY: What did it taste like?

EMILY: It tasted like a body.

KEN: Like a body? Not like real blood?

EMILY: I only tasted the bread, and it tasted like a real body, and you know what? Before they killed Jesus, they took a lot of thorns and they tied them together and put it on him.

TERRY: No, they wrapped the thorns around Jesus' head.

EMILY: Like a crown.

TERRY (*making a circular motion around his head with his finger*): No, like a bandage.

ME: Why did they do that?

EMILY: Because they were afraid of him.

TERRY (*shaking his head*): No, they weren't!

ME: I think they were frightened.

TERRY: No, they weren't. They were mean.

EMILY: They were frightened because they weren't thinking about love, and Jesus was.

ME: Why do you think they put the thorns on Jesus' head, Ken?

KEN: Because they weren't solving problems?

ME: That's for sure. Do you know what thorns are?

KEN: No, but I know it's nothing good.

TERRY (*getting up and sitting down next to Ken*): They're some things that could really stick you, that grow on roses. They're like little needles. If you grab them, they could scratch your hand. They made a crown for Jesus out of them.

ME: Why do you think they did it?

TERRY: Because they were mean, I told you, and they wanted to kill him because they thought he was mean and bad.

ME: Do you think they thought it would make him good if they killed him?

TERRY: Yeah. They put metal wrappers on his hands to get him on the cross. They had to put nails *through* his hands *and* feet. They had to nail him on the cross!

KEN: They nailed him on the cross?

EMILY: Sure. That's what killed him. Yes, it was because God really loved Jesus. He made him rise again in three days.

KEN: What does that mean, "He made him rise again"?

EMILY: It means rise as he should be.

TERRY (*nodding agreement*): It means he came back to life.

KEN: You mean he was dead, and he came back to life?

EMILY (*vehemently*): Yes.

TERRY (*like a preacher*): That's right, rise! The priests say that Jesus has died, Jesus has risen, but there's another name for Jesus; it's Christ. They say, "Christ has died, Christ has risen, Christ will come again!"

ME: Do you think that's true?

EMILY and TERRY (*together*): Yes. [Ken drew a picture of a devil with pointed teeth.]

ME: What do you think he would do if he came again?

EMILY: I don't know.

TERRY: I do, they'd kill him again.

EMILY (*thoughtfully*): You never know when he comes. He comes once, every single year . . .

ME: What do you think about those Bible stories?

EMILY: I dream about them all the time. I dream the same thing happened to me that happened to Jesus, except I didn't rise again.

ME: What happened to you in the dream?

EMILY: They put a crown of thorns all around my head, and then they nailed me on the cross, and then I died, and never came back to life.

ME: That's a very scary dream. Did you tell your parents about it?

EMILY: I used to, but now, never. Never!

ME: Why not?

EMILY: Because they say, "Go back to sleep, nothing's wrong," even after I told them I died in the dream.

ME: You're probably afraid that could happen to you, and I think you're asking why people are so cruel to each other.

EMILY (*shouting*): I had that dream a hundred times! [Her eyes fill with tears.]

ME: A *hundred* times? Really?

EMILY (*wiping at her nose with the back of her hand*): I had it lots of nights for a whole year, after I heard the story about Jesus.

ME: I'm sorry to hear that. Would you like me to speak with your parents about your dream? Maybe you can solve the problem together.

TERRY: Wait a minute, I want to ask you something. Why do people say, when they're mad, 'I'll kill you?'

ME: Why do *you* think?

TERRY: Because they like to kill. In the Bible, the righteous killed the bad ones—righteous means right!

ME: And the bad ones killed the righteous, too, didn't they?

EMILY: They did. [after a pause] I tell my father I'm going to kill him sometimes.

ME: That's because you've heard people say that, and you want to understand why people threaten and hurt each other.

EMILY: No, it's not: It's because I hate him!

ME: Do you think you hate him all the time?

EMILY: No, only when he won't listen to me. Mostly I love him.

ME: I don't think you hate him. I think you're frightened when he and your mother can't listen to you. I said "can't," instead of won't, because the idea of what happened to Jesus, and the thought that you're so sad is so frightening to them that they don't know what to do. That's why they tell you to go back to bed.

TERRY (*after singing loudly*): Goddamn you! Aren't you going to answer my question, or are you just too stupid!?

ME: I'll try to answer it. When people say, "I'm going to kill him," they're afraid someone will kill them, or maybe someone they care about.

TERRY (*impatient, begins to sing louder*).

ME: I'm doing the best I can, Terry. If there was a simple answer to your question, everyone would know it, and maybe they would stop killing each other. Why are you singing?

TERRY: I'll stop singing. You keep talking.

ME: O.K. When people say, "I'll kill you," they're asking questions about why people kill each other. They don't know how to use their brains to solve problems, because saying, "I'll kill you" never solves any problems, but it can make them a lot worse. Most people have learned that they can make a "bad" person good by hurting or killing them. Of course, they can't, because no one's bad. They can only make them hurt, or dead, not good. That's because they weren't bad to start with. It's people's ignorance that causes them to kill each other, not their badness.

TERRY: If they're not bad, what are they, then?

ME: I told you, they're ignorant, and also frightened when they threaten and hurt each other. Do you know what threaten means?

KEN: Sure. It means I'll kick your ass, you don't watch out!

ME: That's right. That's a good example of a threat. Someone who threatens is saying, "I'm frightened by what you're doing. I think it could hurt or kill me, or other people, and that makes you bad. I'm going to hurt you if you don't stop, and that will make you good."

KEN (*flashing an understanding smile*): Like when you whip somebody with a belt, that doesn't make them good, right?

ME: Well, it doesn't help them to be friendly or helpful. It just makes them frightened of you. It may make them stop for a while, but then they'll probably threaten you back, if they get the chance.

KEN: Tell my mother that. She whips me with a belt, and she says that makes me good.

ME: You know, you're both problem-solvers. Should we try to talk to her about it?

KEN: She'll whip you, too; she'll solve your problem.

ME: When your mother was little, and she did the things you're doing now—

KEN (*suspiciously*): What things?

ME: What does your mother punish you for?

KEN: Everything. She say she going to beat the devil out of me.

Suddenly, Terry spit in my face.

ME (*yelling*): What did you do that for? What were you thinking when you did that? Can't you remember to ask me your question in words, instead of doing it? [I panicked and had trouble responding rationally to him. All my training told me he was bad, and I should punish him.]

TERRY: You didn't answer my question about why people kill.

ME: Then tell me that. Don't spit at me!

TERRY (*screaming*): I *am* telling you! [He began to shriek and laugh wildly.]

ME (*more calmly*): Terry, please calm down and stop screaming. If my answer wasn't enough, I'll try—

TERRY (*flinging himself into the wall*): I'm Samson, I'm breaking down this wall!

ME: You know you're not Samson; that story may not even be true. [I should have asked him if he had questions about Samson, but he was dissatisfied with my answer to his question about why people kill.]

TERRY (*yelling*): Samson is *real!*

EMILY (*unperturbed by Terry's outburst*): You know, in church sometimes, I think about whether I'll go to heaven or hell. I go to hell in my dreams. Sometimes I think about throwing kids out the window. I don't know whether I should throw them out or leave them in—if I should do something good or bad.

Since both Emily and Terry were obviously so troubled by their religious education I decided to speak with their parents.

"Nightmare is Emily's code word to get out of bed nineteen times a night," her mother, Mrs. Colon, said. "She talks herself into being afraid. She just doesn't want to go to sleep. And please, don't tell her to ask us to listen to all of her bad dreams. We have four other children, and at three in the morning, we need our sleep."

"In fact," Mr. Colon added, "we have a friend who is an educational psychologist. He told us to get Emily out of your class as soon as possible, or she'll fall apart by the time she's eight years old."

"That prediction isn't helpful to any of us," I said. "Did your friend say why working with me would be so destructive for Emily?"

"Yes, he did. Your telling her one thing and our telling her another sets up a conflict for her. She'll be terribly confused. She won't know whom to believe. We prefer that she believes what *we* tell her, not what *you* tell her."

I began to get anxious. An argument wouldn't help any of us, Emily least of all. I didn't think the Colons' interest and mine were ultimately conflicting. I thought we both wanted Emily to be able to think. "Are we telling her such different things?" I asked.

"I think we are. Do you know, she's asking questions all the time now, at home, and very defiantly, too. She says you told her nothing is bad, that God isn't real, and that "fucking" is an all-right word. Well, let me tell *you* something! Some things and people *are* bad." Mr. Colon paused and gave me a significant look. "There *is* a God, and fucking is *not* an all-right word for children, or anyone else—at least not in this house!"

"Mr. Colon, I didn't tell Emily that fucking is an all-right word. I did tell her that she wasn't bad for saying it, and I told her I didn't think there were bad words or good words, but that many people did think so, and she should know that. I think that children are so fascinated with these taboo words because they want to know what they mean, or why people get so shocked and punish them when they ask. They want to know why these words are considered bad, and they ask by using them. I did tell her that I didn't think people were bad or good. I told her people *acted* destructively, which we've all learned to call bad, but that people weren't *born* bad or good. I told Emily that people don't act destructively because they want to, but because they learned to."

"Well," Mr. Colon said, "you told her a number of things that we disagree with. First of all, she's too young for your theology, and secondly, we'll see that she learns whatever theology she needs in church."

Mrs. Colon put her hand on her husband's arm. "There's something else I'm worried about," she said. "I think you're misinterpreting us to her—as parents, I mean. I think you're making us look bad, making her blame us, and I don't like it"—she glanced at her husband—"We don't like it. You're telling her there is no soul, no such thing as heaven or hell."

"I tried to give her the information I had . . ."

"That's not information, that's opinion. That's *your* opinion!

"And the idea that there's a soul, Mr. Colon, isn't that your opinion?"

"It's not my opinion. In the Catholic religion, the existence of the soul is a fact! I don't want you talking to my kid about religion, do you understand?"

"I understand," I said quietly.

"Look," Mr. Colon said, "you're an atheist, right?"

"Let's say I don't think there's a Universal Mind that controls the universe: that I don't think there's a God.

"O.K. that's good enough. How would you feel if you sent your kid to school, of course not a parochial school, and some nutty teacher—no offense—started filling his head with Christian theology. Now wouldn't that—excuse me again—piss you off?"

"Maybe it would, but I'd try to answer the questions he came home with."

"Wouldn't you say anything to the teacher?"

"Sure I would, but I wouldn't forbid the teacher to explore religion with my child."

"You call that exploring?" he yelled. "That's indoctrinating! Well, if there's going to be indoctrination, it's going to be ours, not yours. And another thing: Where do you get off telling her there's no God?"

"I didn't tell her there's no God. I told her *I* didn't think God existed."

"From now on, drop the topic, O.K.?" Mr. Colon said.

"Suppose," I said, getting up to leave, "Emily hears me talking with some other children about religion?"

The Colons looked at each other. "Tell her," Mrs. Colon said, "to ask us. We'll talk to her about it." They both got up, and walked with me to the door. "Listen," Mr. Colon said softly, "I don't want to be harsh, but this isn't your area. You can talk to her about the body, about science, about where babies come from, but not about religion. I can't make that any clearer."

Later that week, I spoke with Terry's mother about his reaction to the Bible comic he brought to school. I told her I thought the stories frightened him.

"I don't know why they should," she said, in a choked voice, "they never frightened me, and my mother read them to me every night until I was confirmed."

"They seem to frighten Terry, though, Mrs. Brenner. Lately, he's been acting out the stories almost every day, and he looks terrified when he does it."

Her hands began to tremble. "Nonsense," she said. "He needs to hear those stories. Children need to learn about God early. I want him to grow up to be a God-fearing man, who knows right from wrong, and good from bad. I appreciate your interest, but I don't think you should interfere."

Sandra, the daughter of the fundamentalist minister, once asked me if I believed in God. I told her I didn't. "Neither do I," she whispered, "but don't tell anyone!"

One day, before Sandra stopped talking to me completely, she sat on my lap and sang me a song.

> The Lord live in Heaven,
> The Devil live in Hell;

You and me, we live the best we can.
Move over Billy Sunday,
Move over Billy Graham,
Make way for a newfangled
Preacher man!

Children need an education in religion which is not a religious education. They should know as much as they can about all religions, about how they evolved, what questions they tried to answer, and which human needs they tried to meet. Children need to learn the positive and negative effects religion has had on history. This would be an education *in* religion, not *to* it.

We should encourage children to ask questions about God. They need as much accurate information as we can give them about the various theories of genesis, like the Big Bang theory, and Heisenberg's theory of the confluence of gases. After that, we should encourage them to explore and develop their own theories and ideas. Since the promise of the avoidance of death is the cornerstone of religion, we need to discuss death with them openly, and try to tell them what we understand about what does and doesn't happen afterward.

If we give children doctrinal answers to their questions in this area, we abort their sense of wonder and contribute to the pervasive cultural tendency to offer rote answers which are, at best, unenlightening and misleading and, at worst, terrifying. We then add to a confusion which makes thinking more difficult and life more puzzling, by isolating our children within a maze of mythology, without a key.

Let's tell them what we think we know, and what we don't know, and then not stand in their way. With our empathetic help, children can be truly free to choose.

8

Children's Fear of Death: The Jester Box

During the Middle Ages there was a limited but steady demand for court jesters. One requirement, besides an almost infinite capacity to absorb pain, was that the jester be extremely small. To insure that they met standards, novitiates were imprisoned throughout their childhood and adolescence in tiny, cage-like cells called jester boxes. Their growth was permanently stunted, and in their late teens they emerged from these boxes, shrunken and deformed, into the sunlight of the court.

What is it that stunts the social and intellectual growth of our children today? Until the ages of six or seven most of them have a light in their eyes, a brightness, a sense of hope and curiosity. But by the time they are ten, or even earlier, this light has usually dimmed or been extinguished.

Is there something that happens to our children which makes them less curious, less alive? I found, in talking to four- and five-year-olds, that the fear of death was never far from their minds. They thought that death was a continuation of life, that the dead person was buried "alive," and that they "knew" what it felt like to be locked in a dark coffin with the cold rain dripping in, and the worms eating them. They knew that death or the threat of death is used as the ultimate punishment. They had learned this from their total cultural experience; from their families, their religion, their school, the mass media, and even the medical profession. All of these institutions implicitly teach that death happens to children who don't conform, who are bad, who don't do as they are told, who don't listen, and who ask too many of the wrong kinds of questions.

This is our children's jester box.

Michael's mother talked with me about her son's fear of death. When he was four, he became aware that animals die. He saw bloody rabbits, chickens, and ducks hanging in butcher shop windows in his Lower East Side neighborhood. At Eastertime he saw young lambs hanging by their necks on hooks.

Michael asked his mother if these were the same kinds of animals he read about in his storybooks. She told him they were. He asked if they were dead, and again, she told him they were. He wanted to know *why* they were dead. His mother told him that people ate meat which came from these animals, and that even though the butcher killed them to sell to people for food, the animals would die anyway when they got old.

Michael then wanted to know if he would die when he got old, and would his mother and father die, too. His mother said that they all would die eventually, but not for a long time, not until they were very, very old.

"Like Grandpa and Grandma?" Michael asked.

"That's right," his mother said.

"You mean they are going to die soon?" Michael asked.

"Not very soon, but someday."

"Well, then," Michael said, "I'm never going to get old!

If everyone has to die, then I'm not going to get even one day older. I'm going to stay four forever!"

"I'm afraid you can't help it," his mother said. "Everyone grows older, and eventually dies."

"Not me," Michael said. "You'll see. . . ."

A few days after he first saw the dead animals hanging in the butcher shop, his mother took him to Grand Central Station to watch the trains pull in and out. It was his favorite way to spend an afternoon, since he loved railroad trains and he wore a blue-and-white-striped engineer's cap wherever he went.

He and his mother were standing on one of the lower platforms, watching a train preparing to pull out, when an elderly lady approached.

"My," she said to Michael, "you must be the engineer, getting ready to drive the big train all the way to Chicago!" Michael looked up at her. He jammed his hands into the pockets of his railroader's overalls.

"No," he said, "not me, I'm just a *little* boy, standing in the station, watching the trains pull out."

My first memory of death was the day Franklin D. Roosevelt died. I was six. People cried together openly in the streets, as if they had lost their father. When I asked why the people were crying, my parents told me that the President had died. I remember going out to the backyard, to a small garden I'd helped plant, and crying as I pulled weeds.

When there were deaths in our family, of aunts, uncles, or grandparents, no one seemed to cry openly, or at least not in front of me. They mentioned these deaths, briefly and matter-of-factly, but no one ever discussed them with me. I was left to figure out for myself what death must be like.

Later on, when I asked questions about death, the adults around me were uncomfortable. "Why think about it?" they asked. "It will only frighten you. It's not healthy to think too much about death."

"But I want to know what it's like."

"Don't you have any school work to do?" they said nervously, "When I was your age—"

After a while, I learned not to think of it. It wasn't *good* to think about it. Why wasn't it good? No one seemed to know for sure, but the implication was that it might make you sick. I never got a helpful answer, nor do most children, when they raise these questions. Attitudes are changing somewhat, but it is still a taboo subject.

When I was a child, the parents of some of my closest friends died but no one discussed the death in their presence. Teachers never alluded to the children's loss in class. It was as if death was something to be ashamed of, that a finger had been pointed at them. I could have understood a sense of privacy on the part of the children, a need to keep their grief to themselves, but that isn't what I sensed. Death was simply not discussed outside of the family, and often not within it.

In my nursery school class, I tried to learn what the children's ideas about death were, and how they were affected by them. I gave them physiological information about the process of life and death, hoping this would reduce their fear that death is a punishment, and a sentient experience. Of course, the loss of people close to us—family, friends, or well-loved pets—*is* very painful. My purpose was not to pretend that death was painless but to demystify death, for them and for me, so that all of us could be less fearful of dying and more capable of living. "Death is not a punishment," I told the children, "even though human beings have used it as the final punishment for thousands of years."

Too often people confronted with the tragedy of others respond by withdrawing. As children, death was something that happened to other people, and probably because we were afraid that if we got too close it would rub off on us, we kept our distance. I wanted to help the children overcome their fear of death sufficiently to reach out to a relative or friend who had experienced the death of someone close. This isn't too much to ask of children, or any of us. Even if we are afraid to reach out to each other, everyone can, and has a need to, when death occurs.

While I was working with the class, Robby's father died of leukemia. Mrs. Aaron, the boy's mother, knew for some months that the prognosis was very poor, but she hadn't spoken with the teachers. When her husband died, she simply informed the school administrator. I noticed that Robby didn't discuss his father's death with any of his classmates, and I hesitated to bring up the subject with him. After two weeks I finally approached Mrs. Aaron and told her that Robby looked withdrawn, sad, and worried. Although he played with the other children as before, he had sudden bursts of crying. I thought that it was cruel to Robby to leave him, like Job, isolated in his grief, but he didn't reach out, and no one reached out to him.

Mrs. Aaron asked me not to talk with Robby about her husband's death unless he mentioned it first. She was fairly composed, and had resigned herself months before the end. I was relieved to know that she and her son talked openly about the death. She said that Robby talked a lot about his father at home, and cried when he did; she didn't want anyone to "pry" at him and cause him further suffering. She suggested that I let Robby make the first move, if there was to be one.

One day, about a week later, Robby made that move. It was after a small group discussion about the human skull and brain. I'd begun working more with individual children, in an empty room when one was available, or sitting on the stairs when one wasn't. Robby was interested in hearing about the brain, so I asked him to come downstairs and solve problems with me. The children had come to learn that problem-solving meant we discussed any problems they had about anything.

"Let's talk about the body," he said.

I brought a model of the brain and skull with us to an empty room, and explained to Robby how the blood got from the heart to the brain, and around the circulatory system. I told him the blood carried oxygen and nutrients to the brain, and explained both these terms. He asked what would happen to a person whose blood didn't bring enough air and nutrients to their brain. I told him that person would die.

"My daddy died," he said.

I wasn't supposed to know, so I said I was very sorry, and asked when it happened.

ROBBY: A long time ago.* He was very sick, but he wasn't old. He went to the hospital, and my mother went, and I didn't get a chance to see him before he died. I think there was stuff in his blood, because maybe they cut it out. Something was wrong with his blood. My mommy said he just gave a little breath, and then he died. [pause] How old are you?

ME: I'm thirty-four. How old was your daddy?

ROBBY: A little younger than you, I think. You know, I think he died from something like a tree.

ME: Why?

ROBBY: Because there was leaves in there. I don't know why.

ME: Robby, the body is made from little tiny things called cells . . .

ROBBY: Can you see them?

* To many young children, all past events are "yesterday" or "a long time ago"; all future events are "tomorrow" or "a long time from now." They sometimes confuse time sequences, as "the day before tomorrow" or "the day after yesterday."

ME: You can, under a microscope. Do you know what that is?

ME: Yes, but tell me about the cells.

I told him as much as I could, and he listened thoughtfully.

ROBBY: You know, when my daddy died, I was very sad, very disappointed. I cried.

ME: I know.

ROBBY (*looking at the model of the brain*): What's the name of that blue thing that runs across the top of the, what did you call it, the cerebellum?

ME: Yes, that's the cerebellum, and that blue thing is a vein, but I don't know the name of it. The big veins and arteries have names. I'll try to find out the name of that one for you, if you want."

ROBBY: No, that's O.K. I don't need to know it now. But there is one thing. . . . Could he be fixed, my daddy, could they save him now? Is there a new life when you're dead?

ME: Some people think there is . . .

ROBBY: What do you think?

ME: I don't think there is, Robby. I think that once you're dead, you're dead forever, but people remember you, they miss you . . .

Tears rolled down his cheeks.

ME: I'm sorry, Robby.

ROBBY: Well if you were just born, and you didn't know this place, I don't think you could get into another life if you didn't like this one. Some people think God is true, and the angels, and Mary and Joseph, but some people don't.

ME: What do you think?

ROBBY: Me? I think this is our life, and we'll have to get to the end of it, then we'll find out. But it's probably true. They're up there in the air. I don't think you can see them really. I think God is everywhere. The air is God. Everything is God. Inside you, too."

ME: What do you think God is like?

ROBBY: I think he's big, and he could grant you wishes. Mine is for a long life, and that I wouldn't look too old, like those old men and ladies with their canes. To be old is to be dying soon. I want to stay a young man. Everybody lives and everybody dies. *I really don't know how life is when you're dead.*

This is what most children and many adults think: that death is an experience they can and will know; that they will know what it *feels* like to be dead. I explained to Robby that we can't experience death, "know" death, because the organ we do our knowing with is the brain, and we die when the brain dies. We can't see, smell, hear, touch, or feel anything because the molecules (which are combinations held together in a pattern, electrically) in our brains have changed, and can never change back the way they were. They are disintegrating, which means changing from being held together to being loosened apart, and when they come together again, they will still be molecules, but they will no longer be in the form of brain molecules.

"You can know what it's like to be dying," I told Robby, "because your brain is still functioning, but not what it's like to be dead, after your brain stops functioning."

Robby asked about how his body worked, and what happened in hospitals. Why wouldn't the hospital let him visit his father? I couldn't answer him; why *aren't* children allowed to visit in hospitals? Is it because it breaks up the routine, and is inconvenient for the staff? I don't know.

Suddenly Robby noticed some scratches on his leg, and asked about them with some alarm. I explained to him what happened to the skin when it got scratched, but reminded him that his body was strong, and his circulatory system could successfully deal with the scratches. Both of us were anxious after talking about his father's death, but I think I was able to help him explore his reactions to it. I gave him physiological information which would begin to relieve fears caused by the misconception that consciousness persisted into death, and this together with open discussions at home, was a start.

There were differences in the questions that four- and six-year-olds acted out after death. The three- and four-year-olds talked more about death itself, and their games reflected a fascination with it as an experience. Older children seem more obsessed with the question of death as a punishment. Their games and stories were more violent than the younger children's. People died in their games after doing something "wrong," while the younger children acted out death as a result of illness, or a kind of sleep.

One summer day, while working with a class of three- and four-year-olds, Terry and Danny greeted me with hugging and kissing, then immediately fell down, spread-eagled on the floor.

ME: What are you doing?

TERRY: We're playing dead. I saw a policeman shoot people on television last night.

DANNY: Yeah. I had a dream where a policeman shot me, but I was with Batman, so he wouldn't let anything hurt me.

ME: Are you asking why policemen shoot people?

DANNY: I know why: because they're bad. But why do the people die? Why don't they get up again?

ME: When people die, they can't get up again. Their brains and bodies don't work anymore.

TERRY: If the bad guys shoot the policeman, does he die too?

ME: If he was hurt badly enough, he could die. Anyone could die if the bullets destroyed their bodies enough.

TERRY: Not me! I'm going to live forever. I'm Superman!

ME: Superman isn't real, Terry. There are only men and

women, boys and girls, not superpeople. Suppose there was no such thing as bad and good people, that there were only people like you, and me, and your mommies and daddies . . .

TERRY: I'm one of the good people!

ME: You mean you don't want to be called one of the bad people?

DANNY: That's right. We're never bad!

ME: I think you're never bad, too.

TERRY: We're always good!

ME: I don't think you're either good or bad. You're problem-solvers, because you each have a brain.

DANNY: You have to be good or bad, so you know who's supposed to get it.

ME: Get what?

DANNY: Get killed, stupid! If you're bad, you get killed, but only if you're very, very bad. If you're just regular bad, you get spanked.

ME: What else?

DANNY: Sometimes your daddy, or the teacher screams at you. [He and Terry giggle, covering their mouths like the muppets on "Sesame Street."]

TERRY: Yeah. That's when you're stupid, stupid!

ME: You're saying the word stupid a lot, Terry. What does stupid mean? What's another word for stupid?

TERRY (*giggling, but looking anxious*): Stupid, doodie, fuck, shit-ass, monster, dummy, bad, shoot you . . .

In the moral theory that the children learned—to be stupid is to be bad, to be bad is to be in the wrong category, to be in the wrong category is to be in danger, and to be in danger means you may be punished with exclusion and ultimately death.

Look at the traditional methods of punishing young children. When I was in kindergarten and the first grade, "troublesome" children were excluded by being made to stand in the corner, stand in the hall, go to another classroom, go to the principal's office (the worst threat of all), and were even shut up in the clothes closet. Each of these punishments symbolizes the community's turning its collective back on the child, as if that child, because he was bad, had no needs the community (in this case the teacher) was responsible for meeting. Someone's "badness" relieves us, sometimes temporarily, sometimes permanently, from meeting the needs of the bad ones, whether they are strangers, our friends, our pupils, or even our own children.

Later that same afternoon, Ann and Beth fell on the floor.

ME: What are you doing, Ann?

ANN: Playing dead.

ME: What's it like to be dead?

BETH: We can't talk about it. Somebody hammered our mouths shut.

ME: Did you see or hear that somewhere?

ANN: We just made it up.

ME: Are you sure you didn't see it on television, or that someone didn't tell it to you?

ANN: We made it up!

ME: Did you ever see a dead person, Ann?

ANN: No. [Acting as if she's not listening, she begins to walk away, then falls down again.]

BETH: Don't talk to us any more about being dead. We don't like it!

ME: I won't, if you don't want me to, but I'm trying to help you with your fears about dying.

BETH: I'm not afraid.

At this point they tried to get Kevin to lie down and act dead, too. Their breathing came hard and quick, and they began talking in loud, hysterical voices. Had I added to their fear, in trying to relieve it? I felt a sense of relief in speaking about death openly with them, but did they? I was still ambivalent about violating a taboo.

Maybe Beth and Ann's question was, "Can you talk when you're dead?" but I didn't hear it at the time. If that were the question, I would have answered, "You can't talk, walk, think, run, or *do* anything when you're dead." Then I would have explained the change in brain physiology to them in simple terms, whether using books, pictures, or models. I had done this before, and months after getting this information, many children were able to recall almost all of it.

Danny showed me his burn scars on the very first day of school. Six months before, a boiling teapot had fallen on him. He was rushed in a taxi to the hospital, where extensive skin grafts were done. Although the scars covered most of his chest, and part of his back, he showed them to me, Marilyn, and the other children without any embarrassment. Active and curious, Danny loved to learn what held things together, and to build intricate structures with blocks. He was cautious, however, afraid to do anything that might touch his scars, even though they appeared to be completely healed.

We frequented a playground next to a parking lot. Danny usually sat on a bench facing the lot, and talked continually about taxis, ambulances, and fire engines. He brought toy cars and ambulances to school, and banged and crashed them together incessantly. "When I got burned," he said, "I went to the hospital with my father. When I was there, I saw lots of ambulances that said *St. Anthony's* on them. He was crayoning an ambulance in his coloring book. "Now, last night," he went on, "I saw this TV show where a plane fell out of the sky and everyone got killed. They took them to the hospital in an ambulance."

Danny was asking questions about accidents, ambulances, and death. At the sound of sirens, particularly the noon whistle, he put his fingers in his ears. His need to talk about his own accident was so obsessive, because the experience was both so new and so traumatic. Fortunately, his parents had given him a lot of information about it, and I followed through by explaining the physiology of skin and scar tissue, the healing process, and the function of ambulances in emergencies.

Danny was trying to understand and deal with how close he thought he came to dying. One day, at the playground, he heard a fire engine siren, and put his fingers in his ears.

DANNY (*dismayed*): Oh, no, not another one! [then quickly] I'm not afraid of sirens!

ME: Not even a little bit?

DANNY: Yes. A little bit.

ME: Do they hurt your ears?

DANNY: No.

He, Laurie, and Terry began to play "fire engine." (I learned later that Terry had also been burned, though not as badly as Danny, when a cup of hot coffee spilled on him.) Suddenly a real fire engine went by, siren wailing; Terry and Danny shrieked with excitement but they both looked terrified, and Terry started to hit out at the other children. I picked him up. "Are you frightened?" I asked.

"Yes. Yesterday I fell off a high wall, and I had to go to the hospital to get an injection."

"What were you afraid of?"

"Of falling, and of the injection. Look at my injection."

I didn't see either the scratches or an injection mark. I couldn't tell whether this really happened the day before, some time ago, or whether he only feared it would, though it hadn't happened yet. Terry's fears of being hurt and of going to the hospital were triggered by hearing sirens. His scars were both visible and invisible.

It was often difficult to verify children's accounts of injuries and accidents. Were they real events in their lives, or events they feared would occur? Most of their parents worked, so the children were delivered to school and picked up by a constantly changing group of baby sitters, relatives, and parents' friends. When a child told me a particularly painful story about an accident or injury, I would phone parents to try to find out what had really happened.

As I mentioned earlier one of the children's prevalent fantasies was invincibility, superhuman power, and the idea that it would give them immortality. One rainy day, when the classroom was unusually quiet, Evelyn climbed into my lap while I was trying to tie my shoe. She wore overalls and a brown turtleneck sweater that highlighted her soft brown skin and shiny hair.

EVELYN: Don't tie your shoes, tie mine. Besides, I want to tell you a secret. I'm not ever gonna die, ever. I'm magic.

ME: Really?

EVELYN: Maybe not really. [We sat for a moment without talking.] What does it mean to be dead?

I began to answer her, and she started to hit me.

EVELYN: You don't even have to tell me. I'm Supergirl. Supergirl doesn't die, ever. [She pulled my hair, and kicked me in the leg. As gently and quickly as I could, I uncurled her fingers from my hair, and held her foot as I spoke.]

ME: I know you have questions about hurting people, but please put them in words.

EVELYN: If you're Supergirl, you never die, and I'm Supergirl! I get to make other people die, if they're bad like you.

ME: Me? Why am I bad?

EVELYN: Anyone who Supergirl hits is bad.

ME: But why does Supergirl hit them?

EVELYN: Because they're the bad ones! I already told you. Now stop asking questions!

Another time, Evelyn told me she had secret powers to make herself invisible. "There is something about my eyes which makes me powerful," she said.

ME: Your eyes are very nice and brown, but I don't think they're magic. Why do you think so?

EVELYN: Don't be a rotten egg. I saw it in the cartoons.

ME: What happened in the cartoons?

EVELYN: Shut up! I have a pill that gives me power.

ME: Did you see that on the cartoons also?

EVELYN: That's right, Mr. Fuckhead. This pill makes you live forever.

ME: You're asking me one question after another, about what death is, about whether you'll die, about superpowers, and about magic. Even about why people call each other names, like you just called me.

EVELYN: Well, just answer them one at a time, dummy. [She made herself more comfortable in my lap, and made a pretend-angry face.] And you better be right, or you'll get it . . .

ME: One at a time: I've told you what I think death is, and isn't. I don't think you'll die for a long, long time, but if you do, it won't hurt, and you won't know you're dead because your brain is what you know with, and your brain stops working when you die.

As far as superpowers, nobody has them. Some people are very strong, but they die, too. We all will. There is no Superman or Supergirl, if being Super means you never die.

About magic; there's no magic that can make you live, and none that can make you die. People use the word *magic* to describe what they don't understand.

EVELYN: Is that all?

ME: I wish I knew more. I'm just beginning to hear the questions. I'm like you; I'm looking for the answers, too.

I knew how Evelyn felt about not wanting to die. When I was about nine, I prayed every night that neither I, nor anyone in my family would ever die. Since we learn about death as an experience to be avoided at all costs, it's understandable that magical invincibility is hoped for, prayed for, and invoked.

The superheroes, like Superman and Batman, are the good invincibles, who punish the bad people so the good people can live. The children said you could tell who the bad ones were by seeing whom the good ones punished. The bad invincibles were witches and ghosts, but they punished good *and* bad people, particularly children.

One day, Eddie screamed at Evelyn, and jumped on her. His body shook as he swung at her. I moved in to separate and comfort both of them.

ME: What happened?

EVELYN (*crying*): Eddie hit me because I told him I was going to be a witch for my Halloween costume.

ME: (*to Eddie*): Is that what happened?

EDDIE (*very agitated*): Yes. I don't like witches!

ME: But there aren't really any witches. Evelyn is just going to wear a costume.

EDDIE: I don't care. [He tries to hit Evelyn and then me.]

ME: Do you feel frightened, Eddie?

EDDIE: No. Never. [then, quickly] Why do people put razor blades in apples on Halloween?

ME: Where did you hear about that?

EDDIE: There was a story on the news.

ME: What do you think?

[It's a good idea to get as much information as possible about what children think before trying to answer their questions].

EDDIE: I think they do it because they don't want children to bother them. They want to be left alone. What do you think?

ME: Eddie, I don't know, but the person who did that must be very frightened and worried that he or she is bad, evil, and that he'll get punished for doing it. People learn that Halloween is the time when evil spirits come out. Maybe they're asking a question about why people hurt each other, or maybe they knew someone who hurt children that way when they were little, and they're trying to find out why.

EDDIE: I'm not scared of them. I've got magic power and X-ray vision. They can't kill me. I could look inside the apple to see if there's any razors in there. Besides [tears welling up in his eyes], those things just shouldn't happen! If they do, I'll just have to dream about them, and I'm afraid to dream I'll die."

One afternoon, Terry came to school looking very worried.

TERRY: Do you know what a madman is?

ME: What?

TERRY: A madman could kill you!

He kicked at me, and missed.

ME: Are you asking me if that's what madmen do, or if you're a madman?

TERRY: That's right. Am I a madman? Could I turn into one?

ME: I'm glad you're beginning to put your questions into words. No, you're not a madman, and neither is anyone else. That's just another way of saying someone is bad, or crazy, when they're really very frightened.

TERRY: I'm not sure.

ME: Well, instead of using their brains to ask these questions, and working with other people to solve these problems, they are so frightened from being taught they are bad, and will be punished for it, that they go around doing the things they have been told are bad. They've been taught they *want* to hurt other people, but nobody wants to hurt other people, or wants to feel they can't stop themselves from doing things they might get punished for. In fact, the reason they do hurtful things is to see if people will say they are bad, and punish them.

And that's what happens most of the time. People *do* say

they're bad, and do punish them, but that doesn't solve the problem, it just makes it worse. It makes them more afraid that if people think they're very bad, too bad to be saved, they'll punish them with death."

"I still don't know why the government makes war and drafts boys," Richard said one afternoon. He was worried about being drafted. "Maybe it's because you always have to kill the bad guys, so they won't kill you."

ME: Maybe they think *they're* the good guys and they have to kill us because we're the bad guys."

RICHARD: Well . . . they're wrong. If you're good, you live, right? And if you're bad, you die?

ME: I don't think so, Rich. I don't think there's any good or bad, and I don't think you die for being one way or the other. Everyone dies sometime, but it's not a punishment, even though it's often used to punish.

RICHARD: But dropping bombs on people *is* a punishment. And so is war!

ME: That's right, it is, but if people learned that death *wasn't* a punishment, maybe they would stop using it to punish each other.

RICHARD (*his eyes shining*): Do you think so?

ME: Most of the time I think so, Richard. Anyway, I hope so. [Richard seemed relieved, but he wasn't convinced that death was inevitable.]

RICHARD: Listen, I've got an idea to stop people from killing each other in wars. We'll use rubber bombs, and rubber sidewalks, so the bombs will just bounce, and nobody will get hurt. Then nobody would die. Ever.

9

The Last Day of School

As we have seen, the children in my school spoke of death and killing frequently and with great fear. My own fear of death took a different form. Much of the time, I was unable to talk about it with them, and I simply couldn't answer the questions they asked and acted out for long periods of time. I was too frightened myself, too numbed by what I saw and experienced. I tried to recall my experiences as a child, and that was helpful, but I often found myself reliving these experiences, and that was depressing. I even experienced a "school syndrome"; a wiped-out, nodding blur, what Kurt Vonnegut has called "weatherlessness." Heat seemed to numb me. In all seasons, the heat in those old stone buildings was oppressive. The rooms felt hot and still, though they were filled with the sound and presence of children. The noise faded in and out in waves. Everything became hazy, fuzzy. At first I was conscious, but then I began to doze, to nod.

My head would slowly droop down, and I'd pull it up, sharply. Often, I awoke from these brief, fitful naps with a headache. Though I was fascinated, learning about children and myself, I longed to be somewhere else; anywhere else. Marilyn thought I must be reliving the year I spent in nursery school as a child. She said she experienced that same dull ache all through school. Maybe all children have this experience. Possibly all parents reexperience it as I did when I watched the children go through it.

To a child who watches hours of violence and murders on television, and is morally categorized by his parents, his friends, and everyone he depends on, school should hopefully be the place where all this gets explained; but it isn't. Later on, when children are forced to sit for hours at a time, forced to memorize information which has very little to do with reality, when their questions about the world and themselves go unanswered, they escape into daydreams and fantasy. They withdraw, they tune out. If the environment becomes too oppressive, too unresponsive to their needs, they go into school shock, as I did.

Besides the heat, there was the noise. Twenty-two children, four and five years old, in one room for three hours. Little children have an added disadvantage in making themselves heard and understood. Their mouths reach only to adult's waists, so they have to talk even louder. In fact, they have to yell to be heard above one final, universal disadvantage; no one listens.

In the end, I tried to do too much. I'd hoped not only to explore the extent of fear in young children, but also to help them to overcome it. Just identifying the problem, and describing it, doesn't seem enough now. When children confronted me with their fears of death, I sensed my own emerging. I, too, needed to know what they needed to know; about first and last things; about birth and death. I was barely a step ahead of them.

I found that I shared some of the children's problems about teachers. I still looked for approval from them, just as the children did. I was afraid to be in the wrong category; afraid that the teachers wouldn't think me a good person. I violated taboos by teaching children about their bodies, about sex, about death, and by answering questions about God and religion. Would the teachers and the administrators punish me for this? Would they or the parents tell me to leave?

I violated another taboo by working in a nursery school. What was I, a man, doing there? I imagined I heard this unspoken question from the women teachers, and it was a question I asked myself often. In all the nursery schools I visited, I rarely saw a male teacher. At parties, strangers I spoke to about my work asked me, "Is that a job for a *man?*" I learned from the children that teaching in a nursery school is a job for anyone who wants to deal with meeting human needs directly, and a job for anyone who wants to see cause and effect in their work. Teaching young children should not be "for women only," but until we radically revise our awareness of women, and of children's capacity to learn, most men and women will continue to think of this as custodial work. To most men, teaching in a nursery is "only" women's work.

I constantly fought not to be judgmental, but didn't always succeed. One day, Vinnie and Ken argued over a wooden block they were using as a gun. Ken wouldn't give it back to Vinnie, but Vinnie had used it first. Without thinking, I snatched it away from Ken. He was furious. He kicked me and Vinnie, and began to throw blocks around the room.

"How spoiled he is!" I thought, and then stopped myself. If "spoiled" means that a child gets what he wants, it didn't apply to Ken. He had almost nothing he wanted or needed. He wanted to be with his mother more than anything else, but she worked and went to school, so he was in school all day, too. He also wanted friendship, but he frightened the other children so, and was so afraid of them, that he had no friends. Spoiled couldn't mean ruined, because no child is ruined, but many are heavily damaged. I was impatient with Ken, and though I loved him, I gritted my teeth and clenched my fists when he hit his classmates and me.

Once he came into class yelling, "Fuck-off, fuck you!" to all of us, but particularly to Alan. Marilyn said to him, "If you keep talking that way, I'm not going to be glad to see you, because I'm going to be afraid that you'll hurt someone's feelings, or my feelings."

"Yeah?" Ken said, "then I'm getting the hell out of here!" He didn't leave, though. Instead, he followed Marilyn around, asking her, "What will you do to me if I don't do what you say?"

"I won't do anything. I just won't be happy to see you."

"But, my father says 'fuck' all the time," Ken said. "People are always happy to see him."

The truth was that we weren't always happy to see Ken. He left a trail of tears, torn drawings, and bloody heads, but we were all committed to not punishing him, or anyone else, and to hearing and trying to answer the questions he acted out.

Ken often acted out many of his questions at once. One day he knocked down a block building Mike had made. Then he threw the blocks, and tore up some children's drawings.

Suddenly, he turned to me. "Are you mad at me?" he asked.

"No, I'm not," I said, "and I won't punish you. I think that's what you're asking me."

"That's right," Ken said.

"But it frightens me to see you hurt other children, or yourself," I told him. "I think it frightens you, too."

Ken began to hit himself in the head, very hard. I reached out quickly and held his hands.

Eddie walked by. "Hi, Ken," he said.

"Hi, fuck!" Ken answered, struggling to free his hands. "Let me go!" he yelled, "I want to knock down Eddie's building."

"I don't think you do," I said. "I think the idea is there in your head, but I don't think that necessarily means you *want* to do it."

Ken spit in my face, and my arms tightened around him. Both of us were straining, breathing hard. "You mad yet?" he panted. "When will you start hitting?"

Suddenly, he slipped out of my arms, swooped down, picked up a block and flung it into Alan's building with his usual accuracy. Alan and Mike watched him patiently, as the blocks crashed to the floor.

"Come on, Ken," Mike said, "we want to be your friends."

Ken put his hands over his ears. "I don't believe you. Nobody wants to be my friend. Everybody in here hates me!"

He sped around the room, his hands over his ears, shrieking.

He ran out of the room, down the stairs, and then back up. He kicked me in the shins.

"That's what you get for lying!" he said.

"What lie?" I asked, rubbing my leg and biting my lip, and wishing I'd chosen some other work.

"You said you'd never punish me."

"But I didn't punish you," I said.

"Not yet, but you will."

I wondered when, if ever, I would pass Ken's test.

His violence and destructiveness to the children and their work soon reached a peak. Erica, the school administrator, told us that many of Ken's classmates' parents had complained about him, and that she was thinking about asking Ken's parents to withdraw him from the school; in effect, expelling him from nursery school.

Marilyn and I strongly disagreed with her. Though he still had his difficult days, Ken's violence had finally peaked, and had begun to diminish. We could see him changing, becoming less afraid. He'd even started to make friends.

Erica arranged a meeting with the Petrys—Ken's parents—Marilyn, Glenda, herself, and me. It went very badly. The situation put the Petrys on the defensive, though no one wanted it that way. They knew the administration was considering expelling Ken, and possibly because he was so threatened, Mr. Petry felt compelled to defend his practice of beating Ken, severely and regularly. The meeting ended in a deadlock, with Erica frustrated and indecisive, the Petrys frightened and resentful, and Glenda, Marilyn, and I apprehensive for Ken.

As a last resort, Erica decided to call in an eminent child psychiatrist who was also a psychoanalyst. She told us that his report would determine whether Ken stayed or went, and that the doctor wanted to speak with us before he observed Ken. He wanted background material; our impressions of the boy's behavior.

The doctor was a short, heavy man in an expensive vested blue suit. He puffed on an unlit pipe as he spoke with us, constantly nodding his head. He had a sympathetic, gentle expression, but didn't seem to hear when Marilyn and I differed with him. He appeared to brush right past our differences.

"What do you think of the way Ken has been acting?" the doctor opened. He looked intently at me.

"I think he's been doing much better," I said.

"Much better than what? What did he used to do?"

"He used to fight a lot and tear children's work. He still does some of that, but not nearly as much. . . ."

"And you," the doctor said, turning to Marilyn, "what do you think?" "I think he's very frightened, but he's making real progress. He seems calmer, less anxious. . . ."

"Does he seem to you to feel that everyone is picking on him, trying to hurt him?"

"Sometimes," Marilyn said.

"But it's really just the other way around, isn't it?" He puffed on his unlit pipe.

"Yes," I said, "he's so afraid of the other children that he hits them first, but it's his parents behavior toward him that's so confusing to him. He can't understand why they beat him and tell him he's bad one minute, then hug him and say he's their baby the next. It seems to me that he hits because he gets hit. . . ."

"Of course," the doctor said, filling his pipe and not listening. "Well, let me spend some time watching him. From the way I interpret what the administrator tells me, the child is probably delusional and paranoid; probably schizophrenic, but," he paused to light his pipe and look significantly at us, "of course, I always see the patient before I make a diagnosis."

"Then paranoia was the administrator's diagnosis, not yours?" I asked.

"No, it was mine, but merely preliminary. I'll have to see him relate to both of you and the other children. Shall we go into the classroom? I'd like both of you to act the way you normally do, and I'll just take a seat in the corner and watch. Don't pay any attention to me. . . ."

"We often have observers, doctor," Marilyn said, a little sharply, "we won't give you away."

"I might introduce myself to the boy before I leave, so I can see how he relates to me. He sounds very disturbed."

"Don't you want to see him first?" Marilyn said.

"Yes, of course. You go ahead. I'll be up in a few minutes."

Neither Marilyn or I said anything on the way upstairs. She spoke first, when we reached the landing outside of the classroom. "It seems he's made up his mind about Ken. I think he expects to see a raving maniac, and if Ken does any of the stuff he's almost stopped doing, he'll fit right into the doctor's psycho bag, and out he'll go." She shook her head. "Can you imagine being expelled from nursery school?!"

"I think you're right," I said. "Are you game to try something to keep Ken here?"

"Sure. What?"

"Let's keep Ken so busy, between you, me, and Glenda, that he won't have a chance to smack anybody, in case this is one of his bad days."

Marilyn tilted her head up to look at me, and smiled. "Is that problem-solving?"

"I guess so. It's preventing worse problems."

She shrugged and extended her hand to me. "Science strikes again," she said, "Shake."

It was one of his bad days. The doctor sat in the corner, puffing on his unlit pipe. Ken threw a block at Alan which just missed the doctor's head. He made a note. Ken knocked Annie off the jungle gym. The doctor made another note. Marilyn and I looked at each other. Ten minutes had elapsed. Ken ran toward Eddie, a long block in his hand. Glenda swung into action. As Ken raced by, her hand shot out, grabbing the block gently but firmly. With her other hand, she spun him toward the book corner, sat down with him, and began to read him a story.

That took ten minutes. Ken got up suddenly, and ran toward me. He grabbed my by the front of the shirt. The doctor began to write. I spun Ken around so that my back was to the doctor, blocking his view.

The noise in the room was deafening, as usual, so the doctor couldn't hear Ken say, "You bastard, you promised to take me to the lumber yard. I'm going to kick your ass for not doing it!"

Ken swung at me, about crotch high, but Marilyn caught his hand as it lashed out, and completing his motion for him, like a judo move, she pulled him into a circle of children who were dancing "Here We Go Round the Mulberry Bush." After Ken's puzzled look faded, he seemed to enjoy the dance.

Ken was all right for about a half hour, when he began to bite Eddie. I pulled Eddie gently aside and, trying not to look obvious, I sat Ken on my lap as I put a cookie in his hand. He began to eat it, blowing out crumbs between bites. At least he was laughing. I spent fifteen minutes, making up a story together with Ken. Toward the end, he asked me suddenly why some people could hear, and some were deaf. He asked if we had any books about how ears worked. I told him which book had that information, and he got it. After a moment, Glenda handed me a note from the doctor.

"Try not to monopolize his time," it said. "Just do what you usually do."

"This is what I usually do," I scribbled across the bottom of the note.

The doctor scowled as he read my answer. He was still looking at it when Ken pulled back his arm to peg a block at Scott. He looked up as Marilyn slid the block out of Ken's hand and on to a building she was making with some of the other children. At the same time, she pulled Ken on to her lap.

The doctor had written no more notes. He got up to go, nodding pleasantly. Marilyn, Ken, Glenda, and I had choreographed an unplanned ballet. The doctor's report to the administrator stated that Ken manifested merely the normal aggressiveness of a four-year-old confronted with sibling rivalry, and that he manifested the merest touch of autism. His recommendation was further observation by the teachers and administrator, but no referral to any therapeutic facility. Nothing was solved; we'd only bought some time, but Ken stayed.

That afternoon, he asked Eddie not to point a water gun at me (Eddie had brought it in to school under his coat). "If anyone tries to shoot you," he said to me, "I'll feather the gun in eighty-seven pieces, and make it a crown for your head."

I constantly wanted to hold and touch the children, to hug and to kiss them, but they rarely showed affection to each other, and only occasionally hugged the teachers. As a child, I was a "kissy bug." I didn't mind being kissed, as many children do, and I liked to kiss some adults.

The teachers rarely hugged and kissed the children first, but some were affectionate if the child made the first move. In the classroom, I followed the teacher's lead, and didn't act on every impulse to caress a child. I tried to remember, though, to touch or hold children who were isolated by sadness, or in a panic, hitting or being hit, or acting out some other form of violence. Often, words alone were not enough: sometimes, they were too much, and the children couldn't bear to hear any words. Then I picked them up and carried them, or held them gently. They seemed most responsive and comforted when I touched them or held them on my lap and talked to them at the same time.

I've sometimes seen adults deliberately ignore a child having a tantrum. Some do it because they don't know what else to do; others do it because they think it's the best way to get the child to stop. Either way, a child suffers.

I found, time after time, that saying "I know how sad you must feel" cut into the playback of the circuit causing the tantrum, and that gently holding them helped to restore a feeling of contact and support. Of course, tantrums were often more complex than this, and not all of them subsided so easily. However, much of the time, just acknowledging a child's fear, and its attendant isolation, relieved children enough so that they kissed and hugged me with relief, or reached for my hand. They were then usually able to return to class and the work or activity they'd been doing.

Sometimes, when an entire class seemed to go berserk—running, shrieking, cursing, throwing toys, hitting and spitting—I didn't feel at all affectionate. Often, the children who didn't participate in the outbreak would cower in the reading corner or in the bathroom. Sometimes I felt like joining them. I then felt a sense of great anger, of fear, and of frustration. In my panic, I didn't know whether to lash out or run out, but I did neither. I tried instead to think about the cause of this anarchy. It seemed a loss of awareness, of concern, of control, and of reason. Though the children were only four and five, I thought I saw them cast the long shadow of the world and their parents, and the foreshadow of the future adult.

I stopped myself from panicking in response to their panic. Why did I think I felt like hitting them, to stop them from hitting each other? I realized I learned this as I played back my own memories, but it took me and the other teachers some time to calm down after one of these group panics.

What caused the group to panic? Usually, one or two children began to act out, and if it was during a particularly tense time, like a rainy day, or just before or after vacation, the class would seem to "catch" it from them. To me, it meant that panic was catching, unless one fought to think. The children picked up the panic from each other, and I picked it up from them.

Months later, in January, I dreamed that I completely lost control and beat Eddie and Ken with a stick. I woke up depressed, thinking the dream was real, and wondering sickly how I could have done that. "The children won't trust me anymore," I thought. "They must be so frightened now. I've disappointed them and ruined my work."

The thought of hitting children who hit other children, or me, often went through my head. "I'd love to smack him," I thought, but I tried to remember that this idea was not necessarily what I really *wanted* to do. Denah Harris told me that it was critically important not to assume that an idea flashing in my mind meant a desire. "All kinds of ideas emerge in our consciousness every day," she said, "but it doesn't follow that because they are conscious thoughts, they are wishes. Many troubling thoughts are ideas that we learned somewhere, which made us afraid of ourselves and other people. We need to evaluate them."

One of the other teachers tried some of the techniques she saw me use. She was the mother of three children, and liked the concept of problem-solving with them. As a Southern Baptist, she'd learned that children who acted fresh, or bad, got punished, but she thought there must be another way.

She said she admired what I was trying to do. She thought I let the children hit me because I was like Job; that I had a great deal of patience, and it was somehow part of my plan to allow myself to be hit, to be a living example of Christian meekness to the children.

It wasn't so. I never planned to allow myself to be hit, but I didn't know how to prevent the children from testing me this way, without direct or implied threats. I could have stopped them with a stern look, or a loud, "You'd better stop that!" or a soft, ominous, "I'll tell your mother."

That probably would have been the fastest way to stop the acting out, but I didn't do it. I didn't, because to do so would have gone against everything I told the children about the nature of punishment; that nobody needed or deserved to be punished, because no one was good or bad, and that they and everyone else could solve the difficult problems which frightened them, and everyone, if they stopped thinking of themselves and others as bad and good. I never learned to say, "You're stepping on my toe. Get off!" without sounding ominous, so I rarely said it.

Amy's mother had told her to stay away from me, and not to look at the nude, plastic models I'd brought to school to teach physiology to the children. Mrs. Grismont was an ardent member of a Pentecostal church, and she was "sanctified." That meant no dancing, drinking, smoking, or singing, and no curiosity about sex or the body from her daughter.

Mr. and Mrs. Grismont were very quiet, gentle people, but after the New Year, Amy began to attack me after class, when she was alone with me and the two other teachers. She ignored me during the school day, but while she waited for her father to call for her after school, she began to curse and pinch and kick me, without any apparent reason. She ignored the other teachers.

I tried to talk to her, but she met all my attempts with increased screaming and cursing, so eventually I stopped. One day, to protect myself from getting pinched again, I pulled Amy to me, and lifted her up in my arms. Surprisingly, she stopped struggling, and began to hug me. She pretended to be frightened, but she wouldn't let me put her down.

After a month of her intensifying after-school attacks on me, I finally was able to make an appointment to meet with her mother. I was worried about Amy. She was very troubled about something she couldn't talk about, and I was concerned about my own angry and frustrated reactions with her for hitting and spitting at me almost every day. As small as she was, her pinching me, calling me a "white motherfucker," and threatening to get her uncle to "cut off a piece of your ass and cook it up," were making me tense and anxious. The old ideas about punishing bad children began to run through my head, and I sometimes felt my fists tighten when she began her after-school ritual.

I asked her mother if she could think of any reason why Amy was acting this way.

"Nothing I can think of," she said softly, "but she does seem a little upset since Granny Eva died. I have five children besides Amy, and Granny Eva was a lady from my church. She was sanctified, too. She took care of my kids while me and my husband worked. Anyway, Granny Eva died suddenly right after New Year's, and my whole family felt like they had lost a mother. My kids kept asking why wasn't Granny Eva coming to the house no more, specially Amy. She wouldn't touch her food for a long time after that. She was Granny Eva's favorite."

"Did you tell the children what happened to Granny Eva?"

"Sort of. We just said Granny Eva died real quick, and she wasn't coming back no more."

"Did Amy or the other children ask you any questions about the death?" I asked.

"No, they didn't ask nothing, and we didn't say nothing. Wasn't nothing to say."

"You said that Granny Eva died right after New Year's Day?"

"That's right," Mrs. Grismont said, looking down at the table. "I miss her so."

"You know, it was right after New Year's that Amy began to hit and kick me. I think that she might be responding to Granny Eva's death. Maybe she wants to know if death is a punishment for being bad, and if I'm going to make her dead for being 'bad' with me. It's so sad and confusing for her, too."

Mrs. Grismont smiled sadly. "I can't understand how she could do you like that, because all the time at home she be talking about how she's going to marry you when she grows up, but that you probably like some of the other girls in the class better than her."

I said before that I had been tempted to teach Amy a lesson. If I was ever glad that I didn't punish a child, and that I allowed someone to step on my toes because I didn't know what else to do, this was it. Doing nothing wasn't very helpful to Amy, but it was a lot more helpful than the way I probably would have responded a few years before.

On the last day of summer school, I read a story about a bear to the children. I was reluctant to read them animal stories, if the stories were anthropomorphic. My parents read me *Peter Rabbit, Winnie the Pooh,* and *Babar,* among others, when I was small, and I loved them. I found though, that all those animals doing things that only people can do, because they have hands and highly developed brains, is very confusing to small children. They tend to take all stories literally.

The story I read them was about a postman, who happened to be a bear. I hadn't read the story first, and though the children listened attentively, I thought I should clarify the confusing ideas in the story. All the animals talked, the dog rode a bicycle and read a newspaper, the otters cooked on a stove, and the seal knitted sweaters.

"What are some differences between animals and people?" I asked the children.

"Dogs have paws, not hands," Terry said, "and their brains are small!"

"Why can't a dog be a mailman?" I asked.

"Because he doesn't have hands," most of the class answered.

"What other reason?"

"Too small a brain!" Terry yelled.

"Could a dog write a letter?" I asked.

"No," Terry said disdainfully.

"Why not?"

"Because," Terry said, "he doesn't have a pencil!"

"It's the last day of school," Annie said, looking worried. "What will you do now?"

"I'm going on vacation."

Annie looked ready to cry. "I'll miss you," she said.

"I'll miss you, too."

"I'm going to be sad not to see you any more," Terry said.

"Steve, I love you," Melinda said quietly, "you helped me."

Later that day on the playground, I learned something important about the effect of my mistakes. Annie yelled for help from the jungle gym. She hung by her arms, six inches above the rubber mat covering the concrete floor. She was afraid to let go.

"Get me down" she screamed.

"Annie," I said, "look down. You're only a few inches from the floor. Just let go."

"No! No! Help me down!"

Instead of helping her down, I pushed her gently. She let go of the bar and landed on her feet, swayed for a few seconds, and fell to the mat.

"You pushed me!" she cried. She turned over on her stomach and wept. She trusted me to help her, I thought, and I let her down. Like throwing a child in deep water, forcing her to swim. Another big mistake, and on the last day of school, too.

I told Annie I was sorry, that I wouldn't do it again, but I underestimated her resiliency. Five minutes later, she was back on the jungle gym, falling the way I'd shown her, yelling, "Look! look! It doesn't hurt!"

I was relieved. I learned all over again from Annie and other children that mistakes *are* part of the learning process, ours as well as theirs. They get incorporated into the process, or rejected if they don't fit. It's not the odd mistake, or two, or twenty that we make with children that hurts them. It's the constant repetition of the same mistakes, our same negative expectations and projections of willful destructiveness, which prevent them from learning to function as problem-solvers.

In spite of our errors, our blunders, and all the unsolved problems, most children survive. They survive diseases, accidents, categorization, and punishment. So did we, but we can learn to see our children through new eyes, with new insight. We can all transcend mere survival. We can learn to solve problems together, and then begin to live.